Leadership books written by so-ca  substantial track record of leadin, plishments abound. Mark Croston He has been successful in a broad i ing from being a long-tenured pastor in a local context to a national director with a global responsibility. He has actually achieved Big Results, and therefore has the credibility to write about what it takes for you to do the same. This book will inspire and inform you to trust God and serve strategically to accomplish more than you ever imagined!

Jeff Iorg, president,
Gateway Seminary, Ontario, California

Pastor Mark Croston is an outstanding leader and teacher of God's Word. His many years of experience enables him to effectively lead with integrity, compassion, and fortitude. In addition, his teachings are always perfectly balanced with humor and conviction, leading people to live a life of trust and obedience.

Omar Giritli, lead pastor
Christ Fellowship, Miami, Florida

Dr. Mark Croston gives a panoramic view of key leadership principles that if embraced will yield big results in Christian ministry. The principles introduced are hermeneutically grounded as he engagingly weaves personal story, history, the arts, and a clear understanding of the social sciences into a must-have resource for kingdom growth.

Dr. Valerie Carter Smith, executive director/treasurer
Woman's Missionary Union of Virginia

Compelling, cutting edge, creative, and Christ-centered are just some of the superlatives to describe Dr. Mark Croston's book, *Big Results Leadership*. As an accomplished local pastor, past state president, and national leader, Dr. Croston has seen and provided leadership at every level. From the first day I met Mark, approximately ten years ago until this very day, he has always had a heart for the Kingdom of God, Christ, and leaders at all levels. In this book, you will discover scholarly strategies and practical principles that can help leaders provide clearer vision, make better decisions, and build more effective teams. With so much going on in the world and in the church, this seminal work provides a leadership blueprint that is intergenerational, interdenominational, and multicultural!

> **Dr. Emory Berry Jr.**, senior pastor,
> Greenforest Community Baptist Church,
> Decatur, Georgia

This book *Big Results Leadership* by Mark Croston provides the reader with a comprehensive analysis and description of the components and meaning of church leadership. The stories and experiences of the author make it inspiring, compelling, and practical. There is a lesson on every page. The nodus of leadership is grounded in the myriad personalities, social backgrounds, and political negotiations inherent in dealing with people in the church and community. Croston adeptly provides the minister and laity with a *vade mecum* for addressing the basics and difficulties of leadership. People of all backgrounds—beginners and seasoned leaders can benefit from reading this superbly written book.

> **Dr. James Henry Harris**, pastor, Second Baptist Church.
> Richmond, Virginia, distinguished professor of Preaching
> and Pastoral Theology, Samuel DeWitt Proctor School of
> Theology, Virginia Union University, Richmond, Virginia

BIG RESULTS
LEADERSHIP

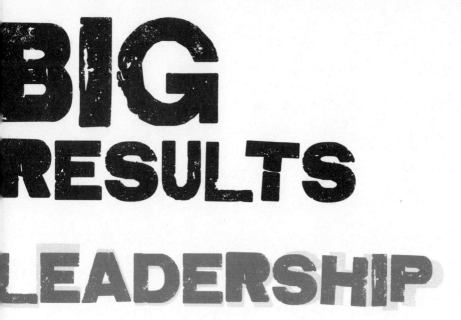

BIG RESULTS LEADERSHIP

MARK CROSTON

B&H
PUBLISHING
NASHVILLE, TENNESSEE

Copyright © 2021 by Mark Croston
All rights reserved.
Printed in the United States of America

978-1-0877-3834-5

Published by B&H Publishing Group
Nashville, Tennessee

Dewey Decimal Classification: 303.3
Subject Heading: LEADERSHIP / PASTORAL
THEOLOGY / EVALUATION

Unless otherwise noted, all Scripture quotations are taken
from the Christian Standard Bible®, Copyright © 2017 by
Holman Bible Publishers. Used by permission. Christian
Standard Bible® and CSB® are federally registered
trademarks of Holman Bible Publishers.

Also used: Contemporary English Version (CEV),
copyright © 1995 by American Bible Soceity.

Cover design by B&H Publishing Group;
illustration by RobinOlimb/istock and MHJ/istock;
author photo by Kayla Holt

It is the Publisher's goal to minimize disruption caused by
technical errors or invalid websites. While all links are active at
the time of publication, because of the dynamic nature of the
internet, some web addresses or links contained in this book
may have changed and may no longer be valid. B&H Publishing
Group bears no responsibility for the continuity or content of
the external site, nor for that of subsequent links. Contact the
external site for answers to questions regarding its content.

1 2 3 4 5 6 • 25 24 23 22 21

Dedication

This book is dedicated to all my fellow ministers of the gospel and church leaders, living here and living in heaven, who have walked with me, poured into me, corrected and encouraged me, shared the burden of the calling with me, and taught me something about leadership.

It is also dedicated to the memory of my father and mother, Rev. Nathaniel Moses Croston Sr. and Isabella Jones Croston.

To my wife, Brenda Michelle Croston, and my children, Candace, Mark Jr., Antonio, and Juliette.

Contents

Preface

I once finished a presentation, and a young man came up to me and asked, "How long did you have to work on that?"

I replied to the young man, "All my life."

Nothing is prepared or completed in a vacuum. I typed the words in this book during the year 2020 in the time of the COVID-19 pandemic quarantine, but they are the overflow of a lifetime of insights and experiences.

I could not have written a word without my mother and father who gave me life, showed me the way to new life in Christ, and provided two excellent examples for me to follow. My father was a pastor in the city of Philadelphia, my mother the church organist. My father died while I was in my first month of first grade. His friends have told me he was a leader and a man ahead of his time. My mother served faithfully as a church musician for more than fifty years.

I was given a tremendous gospel foundation by Ethel Johnson, my first Sunday school superintendent, and Miss Debbie, my beginner and primary class Sunday school teacher. She served our church on behalf of the American Sunday School Union, which is today known as InFaith. One of its urban missionaries, Rev. Howard W. Cartwright Jr., was instrumental in discipling me as a teenager and giving me a passion for the faith.

I am appreciative for all the teachers who taught me. They have all added to my life, but especially Eleanor Peterkins Gross who guided me, Dr. Frederick Branch who pushed me, Dr. Emmanuel L. McCall who enlightened me, and Dr. James Henry Harris who fortified me.

I am indebted to the pastors who shepherded my life after the death of my father: Donald Canty, William Davis, Redfrick Quarterman Sr., William A. Johnson Sr., Thurmond Coleman Sr., and now, Breonus M. Mitchell Sr. Also, to Dr. Clarence James Word who was the pastor emeritus to the East End Church, but like a pastor to me, and to pastor friends too numerous to list.

I am additionally grateful to the churches who have afforded me the privilege to serve and develop as a leader: Liberty Baptist Church, Philadelphia, Pennsylvania; Christian Mission Fellowship Baptist Church, Philadelphia, Pennsylvania; First Baptist Church, Jeffersontown, Kentucky; and Mount Gilead Missionary Baptist Church, Nashville, Tennessee.

I am exceedingly grateful for the East End Baptist Church, Suffolk, Virginia. They took a chance on me as a young man straight out of seminary, who had never pastored anything, and they allowed me to grow and to lead. More than a quarter of a century later, they released me to share these skills and insights with the greater kingdom of God. The East End Baptist Church has become my family; my heart will remain with them forever.

Introduction

What does every leader want more than anything else? I'll tell you: Results! Every leader wants to know their service means something, that their life has not been wasted, that they have not just been marking time or filling a post. Leaders want to leave something behind. They want to gain something for themselves, to do something worthwhile, to advance the kingdom cause. They want to bless God and bless lives. They want to leave things better than the way they found them. They want results!

Some people love the status quo, and some yearn for yesteryear. These are not real leaders. Real leaders find nothing more frustrating than giving all their time and energy to a task that goes nowhere.

All I ever wanted to be was an engineer. One day in eighth grade we had a career assembly. There was a man who had come from what they might call a magnet school today. He talked a lot and showed some slides. But out of the many slides he showed, two highlighted a computer. Sitting in the back of that dark auditorium, I was hooked. There was no music or invitation to come down the aisle. I don't even remember the man's name, but from that day on, all I ever wanted to be was a computer engineer. I went to high school knowing that I was going to be an engineer. I matriculated at the Moore School of Engineering of the University of Pennsylvania to prepare for my lifelong career as an engineer. Following graduation, I entered the world of full-time employment with my dream job at IBM. It did not matter how many hours a week, how many all-nighters or trips, because all I ever wanted to be was an engineer, and I pursued that with passion.

When there is only one thing you can do and nothing else will suffice, it's not just a choice. It's a calling. Some might say there is no such thing as a secular calling, but humor me for a moment and allow me to use this term. In their work "Psychological Success: When the Career Is a Calling," Hall and Chandler suggest one of the deepest forms of satisfaction or psychological success arises when a person experiences labor as a calling, something more than just a job or career.[1] It is to see your work as your life's purpose. God used this to prepare me for my real calling. The one He gave.

Hall and Chandler gave two views of a calling, secular and religious, and they are presented here:

Two Views of a Calling

	Religious View	Secular View
Source of Calling	From God or a higher being	Within the individual

Who Is Served?	Calling serves community	Serves individual and or community
Method of Identifying a Calling	Discernment (e.g., prayer, listening)	Introspection, reflection, meditation, relational activities
The Meaning	Enacting God's larger plan for an individual's life	Enacting individual's purpose for personal fulfillment

From D. T. Hall and D. E. Chandler, "Psychological Success: When the Career Is a Calling," *Journal of Organizational Behavior*, 26 (2005), 160.

Just when everything was going just like I wanted, God stepped in. I was at church the last Sunday in February. The pastor was out of town, and a little old lady named Helen McGowan, our Woman's Missionary Union director, gave a five-minute mission presentation and an appeal for the Annie Armstrong Offering for Home Missions (now the Annie Armstrong Offering for North American Missions). In those five minutes she talked about Jeremiah 1:4–8:

> The word of the LORD came to me:
> I chose you before I formed you in the womb;
> I set you apart before you were born.
> I appointed you a prophet to the nations.

> But I protested, "Oh no, Lord GOD! Look,
> I don't know how to speak since I am only
> a youth."
> Then the LORD said to me:
> Do not say, "I am only a youth,"
> for you will go to everyone I send you to
> and speak whatever I tell you.
> Do not be afraid of anyone,
> for I will be with you to rescue you.
> This is the LORD's declaration.

That day, sitting in the third row on the right side of the sanctuary, God used that little old woman to change my mind and change my life. God tore all my excuses away and gave me His call on my life. I did not tell anyone. I did not cry or shout, but I knew my life had been changed, and I knew what I had to do. I told my pastor when he returned home, and step-by-step I began to pursue this higher calling from God. At the right time, this calling caused me to leave my dream job and move across the country to Louisville, Kentucky, a city where my wife and I knew no one. There I attended The Southern Baptist Theological Seminary as I worked two, and sometimes three, part-time jobs to prepare for my new life's work.

I grew up in the big northern city of Philadelphia, Pennsylvania, the eighth of nine children. My father was a pastor of a small urban church and a supermarket clerk. My mother raised all of us, and after my dad died when I was in first grade, she worked as the dietician of the community elementary school. My siblings and I were the first generation to go to college. Now in a whirlwind, my life had been thrust in a new direction.

God planted me for twenty-six years after seminary to serve at the East End Baptist Church in the small southern city of Suffolk, Virginia. Yes, I had to look it up on a map, too. It is on the southern border, west of Virginia Beach and south of Hampton. It was a small city, urban Baptist church. A highly educated and professional congregation with a Presbyterian-like worship style, steeped in tradition. It was also affiliated with both the National Baptist Convention, USA Incorporated, and the Southern Baptist Convention.

Remember when I said there is only one thing you can do and nothing else will suffice? It is not just a choice. It is a calling. Most people have never experienced a vocational call—not secular and surely not spiritual. A call will force you to do things that do not make sense to those who have been charting their own course. Twice in my life I have received one of these thoroughly disruptive calls from God. The first caused me to leave my dream job at IBM and go across the country to seminary. The second, thirty years later, caused me to leave my dream church, and again to move across the country, this time to work at Lifeway Christian Resources. In both cases many family members and friends could only see these as choices, like they often make their choices. But those of you who have experienced God's call on your life know that this choice has been made for you; and with obedience, whatever the costs, you must follow.

So, why this discussion about calling? I am talking about this because ultimately big results come from a leader who leads. People get into leadership positions for several reasons. Have you ever known someone who filled a spot just because they wanted a title? Maybe they liked the perks (if any) that came with the position, or they wanted something to add to their resume. Maybe they just thought it was their turn. Often people will occupy a leadership position like a maintenance person, doing the minimum necessary. Their goal is to keep the organization afloat, and sometimes their goal is to allow it to sink.

A leader needs a driving force—a call, a passion, a purpose. Leaders need a desire that will fuel their activity because real leadership is not always easy. Traditions, culture, personalities, power struggles, and resources all stand in the leader's way. I have, at times, come home feeling as if I had spent the day pushing an elephant up a hill. Leadership can be exhausting and frustrating but at the same time exhilarating and fulfilling. I think Rosalynn Carter got it right when she said, "A leader takes people where they want to go. A great leader takes people where they don't necessarily want to go, but ought to be."

Mark A. Croston Sr., DMin

PART 1

Study

Everybody has a story. When we don't take the time to know someone's story or worse, create our own version of it, we lose the chance to understand what they need, which is the first step to empathy.
—Jon Acuff, Do Over[1]

Stories create community, enable us to see through the eyes of other people, and open us to the claims of others.
—Peter Forbes

Listen, my son. Accept my words, and you will live many years.
I am teaching you the way of wisdom;
I am guiding you on straight paths.
When you walk, your steps will not be hindered;

when you run, you will not stumble.
Hold on to instruction; don't let go.
Guard it, for it is your life.
—Proverbs 4:10–13

Be diligent to present yourself to God as one
approved, a worker who doesn't need to be
ashamed, correctly teaching the word of truth.
—2 Timothy 2:15

CHAPTER 1

What Did I Just Get Into?

"See what the land is like, and whether the people who live there are strong or weak, few or many. Is the land they live in good or bad? Are the cities they live in encampments or fortifications? Is the land fertile or unproductive? Are there trees in it or not? Be courageous. Bring back some fruit from the land." It was the season for the first ripe grapes.
—Numbers 13:18–20

Numbers 13 tells us a fascinating story. The nation of Israel had been in bondage in Egypt for four hundred years.[1] They cried out to God for a leader who would deliver them. God sent Moses. With signs and wonders, by God's power, Moses led the nation of Israel to freedom, but the Israelites now needed a new home. God gave Moses instructions to lead the nation to the promised land, Canaan.

From Egypt, Canaan was approximately five hundred miles. No one is sure of the exact route Moses took. It could be around 452 miles, or it could be closer to six hundred. So, for a round number, let's just say five hundred. The average man can walk up to twenty miles each day. As a large group they would likely have done less. Let's say 12.5 miles a day. This means they could have gotten to their destination in about forty days. See the simple Google map below from a point in Egypt near the origin of their journey to a point in Israel near their destination. Also, see the note on the left that says, *"This route includes a ferry."* Of course, Moses and the Israelites did not need the ferry because Moses parted the Red Sea!²

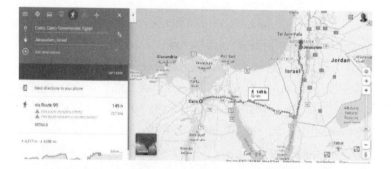

Moses and the nation of Israel get to the edge of Canaan, the Promised Land, but he does not lead them straight in. Instead, as we approach Numbers 13, Moses sends in spies, one from each of the twelve tribes, to bring back a report.

He asks for a Mosaic study[3] of the people, places, patterns, productivity, and profitability.

When they returned, the study team reported that the land was good, really good, flowing with milk and honey. They even brought a sample of the fruit to validate their assessment and made realistic observations about the challenges ahead. We should note that all these observations, so far, were the unanimous consensus of the study team.

Then they did something they were not asked to do. In verses 30 to 33, they went a step beyond their original Mosaic assignment and added a feasibility addendum and their divided opinion about whether they should move forward. Two, Joshua and Caleb, said to move forward and take the land. The other ten, however, assessed that they were too weak and too small, saying, "To ourselves we seemed like grasshoppers."[4]

Years ago, when I was just out of college, I remember hearing Dr. C. Milton Grannum, who had at that time recently started the New Covenant Church of Philadelphia, Pennsylvania, preach on this text about what he called "Valley Versus Mountain People." He said one thing I have carried all my career: "Never decide *what* God wants you to do and *how* to do it in the same meeting." His message was that there are many valley people who cannot see the "how" so they will vote against the "what." It is enough for one meeting just to agree on the "what" and then trust that since God told you *what* to do, He will, at the appropriate time, reveal the *how* as well.

Every group you lead is different. They might have the same name or function as another group, but leaders get into trouble when they fail to first take the time to study those they are seeking to lead. Like Moses' instructions in Numbers 13, study the people, places, patterns, productivity, and profitability. We should add to this list their proclivities. Here are some things to consider.

People

You have probably heard it said that when God made you, he broke the mold. Even though we are alike in many ways, we are not the same. Just as we have been told that every snowflake is different, so are we different from one another. None of us look, think, walk, talk, reason, remember, desire, or do everything exactly alike. There are some people we are more compatible with and others with whom we are polar opposites. From our eyes to our emotions, we are all different.

Our challenge as leaders is to see, understand, and appreciate the differences but build on our commonalities and complementarities. Are they the G.I. Generation, Silent Generation, Baby Boomers, Generation X, Millennials (Generation Y), or Gen Z?

Are their economics upper-upper, upper, lower-upper, middle, lower-middle, upper-lower, lower, or lower-lower? Are they givers or tight fisted? Needy or greedy? Do they wear a blue collar, white collar, or no collar at all? Are they laborers or professionals? Are they paid by the hour, or do they earn a salary? Are they corporate, entrepreneurs, small business owners, or union workers? Do they have careers or jobs? Are they wise or foolish? Investors or debt ridden? Do they have high school diplomas, graduate degrees, trade school, or no school? Are they tech savvy, technically challenged, or tech resistant? And that's only about their work!

Are they single without children, single with children, married without children, married with children, divorced, widowed, separated, adopted, or adopting? Homeowners, multiple-home owners, or renters; single family homes or multifamily units? Do they want to try new things, or do they work hard to keep things as they are? Are they Republicans, Democrats, or Independents; progressive, liberal, moderate, conservative, or ultraconservative? Is their origin European, African, Asian, Latin, or Native American? Is their music preference country, classical, R&B, jazz, rock, or pop? Are clothing styles trendy or traditional, formal or informal, business or casual?

Places

What one does in one place may not work in another place. Some places are demographically different; others have an alternate worship style. Is your place rural, urban, or suburban? Uptown, downtown, or midtown? Small town or big city? The place impacts traffic, travel time, travel costs, and parking.

Passing through the Washington, DC, area on a number of occasions I got caught in traffic for hours, and sometimes it was not even during rush hour. So, do you think this could impact attendance for weeknight events at church, at school, and in the community?

During the COVID-19 pandemic of 2020, many churches transitioned their weeknight Bible studies and life groups to online formats. Many pastors suddenly had more people in their weeknight online groups. Why? Because people did not have to fight the traffic getting home, pick up kids, and get something to eat before they headed to the church. So, while it may be fairly easy in some places to do weeknight events, it is difficult in others.

Patterns

When I first arrived to serve East End Baptist Church, my wife noted right away that they did not have an evening service. She grew up with Discipleship Training (BTU, BYPU, CT) at 6:00 p.m. to 7:00 p.m. and Sunday evening service from 7:00 p.m. to 8:30 p.m. every Sunday. Note that I called this Sunday evening "service" not worship. When we married and I had to leave, I was not always feeling the joy of the Lord on those evenings. Anyway, she declared that all churches had a Sunday evening service, and we needed to start one there right away!

What are the annual, monthly, weekly, and daily patterns? Sometimes we will see something that works in one place, but the patterns of your people will not allow that same thing to work in your location.

It turned out that at this place, one-third of the economy was military or military related. There were bases for every branch of military service in the area, as well as a number of shipyards. This meant that many of the members had to get up early to make it to work before 6:00 a.m. Well, out of necessity, they also went to bed early. So, because of our context, we never did start that Sunday evening worship.

Some years later, sitting exhausted on the sofa with my wife on a Sunday night, I turned and asked, "Aren't you glad we didn't start that Sunday evening worship?" No response.

Productivity

What is the group's productivity? Here is something that taught me a lesson. In the church where I grew up, if there was going to be one of those big famous church dinners, the women were going to handle it, and handle it, they did! There is nothing like one of those old-time church dinners! Fried chicken, collard greens, potato salad, fresh baked yeast rolls, sweet potato pie, and church punch. I have come to learn that every church has their own recipe for their signature church punch. In Virginia our church had sweet tea. Sometimes it was so sweet I would have to get half sweet tea and half water. In my Pennsylvania church, it was always a mixture of grape juice and pineapple juice. The grape just might have been Kool-Aid, but it was good anyway.

I bring this up because when I went to Virginia and wanted to have a big church meal, I asked the women of the church to help cook in the kitchen. If looks could kill, I would have died a thousand deaths that day for sure. It was as if I insulted them just by asking. What I found out over time was that every church's productivity was in a different place.

Unlike my childhood church in Pennsylvania where the women loved the church kitchen, at East End, my Virginia church, the men did almost all the cooking at the church. There was one woman who didn't mind cooking in the church kitchen, Yvonne, but other than her, it had to be the men.

It took me a while, but in time I learned that the women in my Virginia church were not anti-cooking. They were just anti cooking at the church. If I asked them to bring something to the church, they would do it with excellence and delight.

Each group you lead will have its own pattern for productivity. The person or people we think sometimes will do the task may not be the ones who actually will. Assessing the history, skills, and personality traits of a group is important. Avoid putting square pegs into round wholes.

Profitability

Not all groups are profitable. Some like the way they are and the things around them. They just do not want to change. Their favorite song is "Just like the tree, planted by the water, I shall not be moved!"

What groups often do not realize is that you cannot keep things the same no matter how hard you try. Times, seasons, fashion, technology, and landscapes all transition around us. Buildings decay, clothes wear out, people get older.

Think about Moses. Forty years with a grumbling, complaining group, stuck wandering in the wilderness. Some were insistent on going back to Egypt. Somebody might have even asked, "Which way to get back to the good old days?" People who do not want to evolve in positive directions are counterproductive. They romanticize the past and forget that the good old days really were never as good as they remember. Can I quote Alan Bergman, Marilyn Bergman, and Marvin Hamlisch here? The song was first sung by Barbara Streisand and later by Gladys Knight. Do you have it yet? The song is "The Way We Were."[5]

Oh, can it be that it was all so simple then
Or has time rewritten every line.

Numbers 32:13 says, "The LORD's anger burned against Israel, and he made them wander in the wilderness forty years until the whole generation that had done what was evil in the LORD's sight was gone." Wasted time, wasted lives, and wasted productivity.

So Moses spent the forty years of his life roaming around the wilderness and never making it, himself, into the Promised Land. You may find yourself at times in a situation like Moses. In such a case you must pray to God to determine whether that is His assignment for your life. Remember, God does not purpose everyone to be big, rich, popular, or famous, but God does call all of us to be faithful. Big results for God may sometimes look like failure in this world's system. No one would declare Moses a failure; we would declare him faithful.

Proclivities

Every group has its own personality and proclivities. Do not miss this. What works in one place and with one group may not work the same way in another. Why is that?

In one of the Winnie the Pooh cartoons, Tigger, the bouncing tiger, is happy-go-lucky, bouncing around while Eeyore, the donkey, is about to have lunch. Eeyore says to the Pooh: "Could you ask your friend to do his exercises somewhere else? I shall be having lunch directly, and don't want it bounced on just before I begin. A trifling matter, and fussy of me, but we all have our little ways."[6]

Did you notice the ending phrase, "We all have our little ways"? Organizations are imperfect because they are made up of imperfect people. You need to discover whether they are clannish or open to new people? Do the children stay at the church or leave the area when they graduate? Have they traveled the world, the country, or just their state or county?

Do they prefer home cooking or restaurants? Are they stuck in the pain of the past or open for new adventures?

Taking the time to study your organization so you can know who its constituents are is vital. After I had been at East End for about a month, my mother came to visit on the weekend of my installation. By then I thought I knew all I needed to know. As I talked with my mother, I was peppering off item after item, and everything I saw that I thought needed to be updated, changed, uprooted, or fixed.

My saintly old mom stopped me in my hurry and said, "Son, this is the church. It is not the speed boat of Zion; it's the old ship of Zion." I knew exactly what she meant, and I have strived to heed her advice ever since.

An average speedboat may go up to 50 mph. *Problem Child* is the fastest nitro dragboat in the world. It cranks up 8,000 HP and can achieve the speed of 262 mph in an unbelievable 3.5 seconds![7] A modern cruise ship travels at 20 knots (about 23 mph) with top speed of 30 knots (34.5 mph). An average speedboat weighs 8,000 pounds, a cruise ship about 200,000 GT (gross tons), which is about 400,000,000 pounds. So, if you remember your high school physics class, momentum would be a factor in turning either vessel. The applicable equation would include momentum equals mass times velocity. My point is that you can turn a speedboat much faster than a cruise ship.

It takes time to retrain and change the proclivities of a group of people. The leader should take confidence in the fact that if the leader stands at the helm long enough and moves with intentionality, even a group's inclinations can be transformed by the power of the Holy Spirit.

Taking time to fairly assess your situation is the first step toward a productive future. Several years ago I traveled to New Jersey to interview a young pastor who was ready to leave the church he was serving after just two years. In the interview I asked him to tell me about his current church and situation. He went on to share his complaints and frustrations about the people, the place, and the practices. When he finished talking, I slammed my folder shut and declared to him, "This interview is over! God did not send me here to offer you a job but to tell you to stay where you are."

It was obvious to me that the young pastor couldn't see it, but from all he told me I knew what was true. I went on to tell him to stay there, be faithful, and preach the gospel, and the church of his dreams would materialize before his eyes. Years have passed and around the time of his pastoral anniversary, in one form or another, he sends a note that celebrates the fact that he is still standing.

The right assessment of where you are can make all the difference. Studying the people, places, patterns, productivity, profitability, and proclivities can take you where God wants your leadership to go.

CHAPTER 2

Gain a Passion for the People

The Spirit lifted me up and took me away. I left in bitterness and in an angry spirit, and the LORD's hand was on me powerfully. I came to the exiles at Tel-abib, who were living by the Chebar Canal, and I sat there among them stunned for seven days. Now at the end of seven days the word of the LORD came to me.
—Ezekiel 3:14–16

One sunny day a man was driving in his car down a pristine city street. As he looked out the window, he noticed an old friend sitting at a table with a woman. They were staring intently at each other and having what seemed to be an intimate conversation. It just happened that a week later the man in the car got to see his friend at a business meeting. He said to his friend, "I saw you the other day as I drove down Primrose Lane. You were at a sidewalk café, talking to a pretty lady, and what she was saying must have been fantastic because she had your complete attention."

The friend replied, "Sorry, that was not a sidewalk café. That was my furniture on the sidewalk. I was being evicted. That was not just some pretty lady with me at the table; that was my wife. And yes, I was listening closely. She had just told me she wanted a divorce."

How many times have we been wrong about other people? We jump to conclusions based on what we see, filtered by our own knowledge and experiences. I'm convinced that people will most often impose on others what they might have done themselves if ever in a similar situation. So, how many times have we been wrong?

This kind of wrong is different from prejudice. Prejudice is based on one's preconceived stereotypes of a group or type of people. What I am talking about here is more like jumping to a conclusion about another's actions without the benefit of the necessary facts. When we do this, we will often, right or wrong, impose our values and choice patterns on the other person.

A Native American plains proverb says, "Great Spirit, grant that I may not criticize my neighbor until I have walked a mile in his moccasins." In 1895, this thought was captured in a poem by Mary T. Lathrap.

> Pray, don't find fault with the man that limps,
> Or stumbles along the road.
> Unless you have worn the moccasins he wears,
> Or stumbled beneath the same load.
>
> There may be tears in his soles that hurt
> Though hidden away from view.
> The burden he bears placed on your back
> May cause you to stumble and fall, too.[1]

Let's take a moment to gain some biblical insight here from Ezekiel. The book of Ezekiel is one of the major prophetic books of the Old Testament. Ezekiel enters the prophetic scene, according to dates in the text, in the fifth year of the first deportation to Babylonia (592 BC), and he prophesied until about 570 BC. He was among the exiles for the majority of his prophetic work.

The book of Ezekiel opens with fantastic imagery of the earth and the heavens and of the elements and creatures. Ezekiel gave an appropriate response in Ezekiel 1:28: "The appearance of the brilliant light all around was like that of a rainbow in a cloud on a rainy day. This was the appearance of the likeness of the LORD's glory. When I saw it, I fell facedown and heard a voice speaking."

In chapter 2, God gives Ezekiel his assignment. God is sending him to an obstinate, hard-hearted, rebellious group, and he is encouraged not to be afraid or discouraged. In the opening of chapter 3, Ezekiel is encouraged to eat the Word of God, "For you are not being sent to a people of unintelligible speech or a difficult language but to the house of Israel" (v. 5). Yes, he was sent to his own people. Now that's a whole extra leadership challenge we won't address right here, except to say that even Jesus had some extra challenges with people who knew Him from His hometown, Nazareth.

The bitterness and anger in Ezekiel's spirit in Ezekiel 3:14 suggest that he was not in the right frame of mind to lead the people of God. There have been times when, in anger, I have written an email to give someone a piece of my mind. There have even been moments when I have written and prepared a sermon ready to deliver to those who needed to hear it, but in both circumstances God gave me time, got hold of me, and helped me know that what needed to be communicated or accomplished could be done in a less angry and, need I say, more Christian way.

None of us approach our leadership assignments *tabula rasa*, as if we are starting completely fresh with a blank canvas or a clean slate, completely impressionable, on which anything can be written. All of us are a bundle of life's history, our local culture, and our personal experiences. I have often watched leaders try to duplicate something they saw or heard, that worked with some other group, and on the surface looked similar, but it did not work out at all. Digging into the history, culture, and experiences of an organization is more than getting current demographics. It is like exegeting a biblical text to understand the often hidden truths.

Instead of charging right in and impacting everything quickly, wisely, Ezekiel first sits in Tel-abib by the Chebar Canal. He stays there for seven days. The name Tel-abib probably means "hill of ears."[2] This would have been a great place to listen, at this moment not just for the voice of God but to hear, appreciate, and empathize with the cries of the people. He sat there for seven days. The number *seven* typically means "completion or perfection." This says that sometimes we need to sit until we get the message God intended.

At the end of seven days, Ezekiel is stunned, astonished, overwhelmed. This could suggest a need for us to sit, look, and listen long enough to understand, appreciate, and be moved by the plight of the people we serve. They are not there to serve us. We are assigned to serve them by leading and enlightening them in God's way.

Life's History

Surely, we are all impacted, influenced, and even prejudiced by both secular and sacred history. Just digging into that would take volumes by itself. Here let us limit our conversation to the history of the group or institution you are leading.

It's nice when groups have a written history. There are things you can learn by what is said and what is not said. Dates, times, events, places, and names all have significance. In one season our church was asked to lend a historic painting we owned for a display drawing from the local churches at the city's art museum. The final curation was impressive. I had not realized there was so much history around us. One thing I found intriguing was a journal containing a log of a prominent local school's activities. As I recall, it recorded that the school was closed during the week of August 21, 1831, due to events in South Hampton County. Events? So, to what events could the log be referring? A state fair? A tropical storm? Well, it was a storm all right. I did not have to search my memory long to remember that August 21, 1831 to August 23, 1831 were the dates of Rev. Nat Turner's crusade for freedom, justice, and equality. Of course, some history books refer to these dates as the Nat Turner Insurrection.

My point here is whenever reading an organization's history, always remember it is written from the perspective of the writer. Sometimes histories are written as a defamation of the truth and at other times as a eulogy, only extolling the best values and virtues. Use your critical eye to discern the real story behind the recorded facts.

Sometimes the true history is not in the written documents, and you will have to dig farther. One year, while attending my late wife's family reunion, I had a new family tree program on my computer and was thrilled to have all the older family members together so I could fill in some of the empty spaces. On one of the evenings while the younger crowd went out for an event and the old heads remained in place talking together, I knew this was my chance. So I sat with groups of five or six seniors and went to work asking my questions. Boy oh boy, did I get an earful that night! *So and so is not really that one's father. . . . These two over here never got married. . . . This one is related to that girl you see on that show in New York. . . .* My point is that some personal recollections, stories, and oral histories will never make it into the written history, but they are a legitimate portion of the organizational history just the same.

An organization is not just its history and should not be limited by its history, but its history does inform us of important patterns and preferences that may need to be accommodated as you move to the new future.

Local Culture

Cleo TV is a fairly new urban cable television network whose target audience includes African American millennials and Generation X women. They feature a travel, food, fashion, and design program called *Lens of Culture*. Their point is that we can all be looking at the same thing, but we may see it, appreciate it, or even be repelled by it because of our own life experiences. Indeed, even the biblical text is seen through all the rigors of our study and our own cultural lens.

Culture is the collective beliefs and ideals that energize the behavior of a group of people. Culture is passed down from our parents; informed by our media sources; shaped by our faith, our community, and our peers; and solidified by our experiences. The organization you lead may be similar to another, but it has its own unique culture.

Who are the people or families of influence? Why are they afforded this deference? What are the thought-shaping events or influences? Culture over time can be changed, but to run up against it can be like paddling in the wrong direction in a raging stream or using your head to try to break through a brick wall.

My life started in the north, in Philadelphia, Pennsylvania. I was there through my college years and the first years into my engineering career. Then I moved to Louisville, Kentucky. I quickly learned that things were different in the south. People in Pennsylvania, in my estimation, were friendly, but the hospitality in Kentucky seemed so much greater. From my first Sunday in Kentucky to the last, people were always inviting my wife and me to their home or out to a restaurant for dinner. It was fantastic. Then, from Kentucky, I went to lead the church in Suffolk, Virginia, also in the South. I thought Kentucky was my introduction to southern culture and that everywhere in the South would be just like that. Boy was I wrong! It wasn't that people in Virginia were less hospitable. What I found over time was that their hospitality was in a different place. It was shown in a different way. Now that I live in

Tennessee and have traveled to almost forty different countries, I have two observations.

Observation one is this: Everybody is the same and everybody is different. What I mean is that everybody deals with the same basic life issues, but how we lead people through them can be impacted by the culture in which they live. The gospel is great. It works beautifully everywhere, but leadership is done within a culture and is moderated by ethnicity, education, environment, and economics.

Observation two is that local culture is not monolithic anymore. A few years ago, when I was serving as pastor in Virginia, I attended a meeting in Atlanta, Georgia. At the meeting were leaders of twenty-seven ethnic fellowships in the Southern Baptist Convention (SBC). Next to me was the president of the Vietnamese Fellowship. During one of the sessions, he quietly slid a gospel tract toward me. I took one look at it and saw it was written in something I couldn't read. I assumed it was Vietnamese. So I quietly slid it back and said, "We don't have any Vietnamese in my area." He pushed it back to me again and said, "Go to your local nail salon." So, at a meeting in Georgia, a guy from Arizona who had never been to Virginia, told me where to find Vietnamese people in my neighborhood.

I started taking a look around. I noticed more distinctly that there were more than just black people and white people in my city. The owner of the nail salon was Vietnamese. The owner of the beauty supply was Korean. The owner of the motel was from India. My doctor was from Kenya, and my wife's doctor was from the Philippines.

I looked inside my congregation and saw people from Uganda, Ghana, Jamaica, Trinidad, and Saint Croix. There were Hispanics from Panama and Caucasians of Irish and other European ethnicities. I came to realize that our church in a little southern town was looking more and more like the kingdom of God and what heaven is going to look like. While the numbers of the various ethnicities were not great because of the demographic of our community, the openness of our church was great.

How did it happen?

1. **We had a pastor-led commitment to missions.** Since the end of my college days, I have traveled for vocation and vacation in almost forty countries on five continents. Every year for nineteen years while I was at that church, I, the pastor, led one of our international mission trips. This helped me and the members of the congregation to develop and maintain a true biblical worldview and passion for people. Sometimes, we have a biblical view, but it's really a biblical community view.

2. **We led the church as a church that was black, rather than as a black church.** We

were a church that was black because we were in a community that was demographically black. That meant we could embrace and celebrate our heritage as black Americans but at the same time be open to accept and embrace people who were not black Americans. I believe if you hold up your ethnicity over your Christianity you may consciously or unconsciously be closed off from God's greater kingdom work. If we see ourselves as a black church, white church, Korean church, or whatever, it means that all who come to us must conform and become what we have declared we are, but if we see our Christianity first and our ethnicity only as representing the people we currently serve, we remain open to God's leading others our way who may not be what we have been but are a part of God's greater kingdom agenda.

3. **We celebrated every member of the congregation.** We had flags that hung in the sanctuary, but the only flags we hung were those that represented countries we, as a church, had traveled to on mission or countries in which our members

were born. We did international pot-lucks, dressed in the attire of native country Sundays, and we were open to new songs members brought from their homeland or from a mission trip.

We love to pray, "Your kingdom come. Your will be done on earth as it is in heaven."[3] Seeing, appreciating, and being sensitive to the different cultural elements and differences around us is part of making this prayer a reality.

Learned Experiences

Every person has a story. Maybe the assumption is that our stories may differ, but since they are in the past, they do not matter for our present and future. I love the scene in *The Lion King* where Simba, the son of the king, has run away from his life and responsibilities. The wise baboon, Rafiki, finds him, and in a discussion, takes his stick and strikes Simba on the head. Simba says, "Ow! What was that for?"

Rafiki answers, "It doesn't matter. It's in the past!"

Simba insists, "Yeah, but it still hurts."

Rafiki responds, "Oh, yes, the past can hurt. But the way I see it you can either run from it or learn from it."

Our story, our personal experience, colors our perspective and either enhances or limits our response. It increases our success and deepens our struggle. As a leader, you will encounter stressed people every day.

First, don't take every negative glance, word, or encounter personally. Sometimes, you have nothing to do with the other person's obvious irritation; you may just be present for the fallout. One day after a presentation, an older lady, with a grimace on her face, came up to me. In a rough voice but with a wise heart, she said, "I just don't want you thinking that while I'm looking mad out here that it has anything to do with you. My back is killing me, but I wanted to be here, and it was all I could do just to stay in my seat during your presentation."

This story could be told over and over again. An older man had a negative experience with the state police when he was in his twenties. Another whose only memory of his father was when he was a little boy, and his dad tossed him an Indian head nickel as he was about to drive away, never to be seen in his life again. A woman who had been secretly molested as a child and acted out her brokenness through a series of affairs in her marriage. Another man avoided all sick people because several family members died of tuberculous when she was growing up. What about the ones who were bullied, homeless, hungry, orphaned, abandoned, or impoverished? And there are those who have never divulged their demons, but the cracks in their lives are evident.

Ezekiel 3:15 says that the prophet was left "stunned." I imagine as he arrived, he wondered why these people were doing so badly. After sitting there, he was stunned with all they had been through and yet had to deal with the present, wondering why they were doing as well as they were.

Knowing an individual's story helps us understand the awkward things they do sometimes. To some degree we are all broken. Getting in touch with our own story is as important as knowing the stories of those you are attempting to lead.

CHAPTER 3

Find the Motivation

One person believes he may eat anything,
while one who is weak eats only vegetables.
One who eats must not look down on one
who does not eat, and one who does not eat
must not judge one who does, because God
has accepted him. Who are you to judge
another's household servant? Before his own
Lord he stands or falls. And he will stand,
because the Lord is able to make him stand.
One person judges one day to be more
important than another day. Someone else
judges every day to be the same. Let each one
be fully convinced in his own mind. Whoever
observes the day, observes it for the honor of
the Lord. Whoever eats, eats for the Lord,
since he gives thanks to God; and whoever
does not eat, it is for the Lord that he does
not eat it, and he gives thanks to God. For
none of us lives for himself, and no one dies

> *for himself. If we live, we live for the Lord;*
> *and if we die, we die for the Lord. Therefore,*
> *whether we live or die, we belong to the Lord.*
> —Romans 14:2–8

n recent years I have had to learn a whole new vocabulary. I used to think all vegetarians were vegetarians, but alas they are not. According to Mayo Clinic:[1]

- **Vegans** eat only vegetables, but if one is a *raw vegan* then only raw, and no cooked vegetables.
- **Lacto-vegetarians** eat only vegetables and dairy products such as milk, cheese, yogurt, and butter.
- **Ovo-vegetarians** eat only vegetables and eggs.
- **Lacto-ovo vegetarians** eat only vegetables, dairy products, and eggs.
- **Pescatarians** eat vegetables, dairy, and fish.

My wife and oldest daughter are vegan. One son is a lacto-vegetarian. The other son is an ovo-vegetarian. A niece who lives with us calls herself a pescatarian but is really a lacto-ovo-pescatarian. Only another daughter and I continue to eat like Jesus and consume meat.

This all has given me a new appreciation for the opening verses of Romans 14 because people who are walking different paths may not be doing it with the same underlying motivation. Part of my enlightenment in this area is that my family members all arrived at their cuisine selection destination by different processes and for different reasons. None of those reasons were religious. One wants to lose weight; one thinks it is healthier; one has difficulty digesting meat; one has IBS (irritable bowel syndrome); and one has acid reflux.

When leading, knowing what's going on is good, but knowing the underlying motivation is even better. Businesses, churches, clubs, teams, and organizations all have underlying motives for why they do what they do. My first corporate job was with IBM. By the time I came to work there in the 1980s, all the men wore dark blue suits. The IBM logo was blue, the early monitors were blue, and IBM was a leading blue-chip stock company. It was no surprise that IBM was nicknamed by this time "Big Blue." The blue suits were not an accident or some edict by a corporate executive; they grew out of the culture. No one ever told me I needed a blue suit. When I showed up on my first day in a nicely tailored Joseph A. Banks gray suit, I felt like a fish on land.

So what you see in your organization may only just be scratching the surface. Our organizations are like icebergs. When looking at an iceberg, you only see about 10 percent of the total. Conversely, 90 percent of the iceberg is below the water's surface.[2] In the same way, when we arrive at an organization or when visitors come, only 10 percent is really on display.

I have known leaders who saw some ministry or event happening in another church and went back to reproduce what they saw perfectly but wonder why they did not get the same results. That is because they only reproduced the top 10 percent, the surface stuff. They did not reproduce the 90 percent that lay beneath the surface, obscured from the casual viewer's sight.

One thing beneath the surface is the motivation. There are four types of motivation: extrinsic, intrinsic, introjected, and identified motivation.[3]

Response

		Reaction	Inaction
Origin	External	Extrinsic Motivation	Identified Motivation
	Internal	Intrinsic Motivation	Introjected Motivation

Extrinsic motivation comes from the outside. We do it because we are encouraged externally or because we are ordered by someone who has authority over us.

Many employment motivation systems work on the principle of extrinsic reward. This is where people are commanded and then rewarded with things like bonuses or promotions. At times this is useful and even necessary, but it does not encourage people to be self-motivated.

Intrinsic motivation is a response to internal rationales to align with a goal or for the personal satisfaction of doing something.

In churches members are intrinsically motivated by working for an inspiring leader or in areas where they have a personal interest.

Introjected motivation is similar to intrinsic motivation in that it is internalized. The distinguishing aspect of this is that if it is not done, then the person experiences remorse and anxiety.

Identified motivation is where a person understands that something needs to be done but has not yet committed to do something in regard to it.

Like people, organizations over time develop a corporate personality so it is vital for a leader to assess and comprehend the entity's *intrinsic* motivation. Remember this: no two churches are exactly alike. You may be at a church of the same denomination, size, and situation as someone else, but each one has its own personality, fueled by an underlying passion that has been developed over time and through their experiences.

We are all alike, but we are not all the same. This is true with churches, institutions, and organizations. In some ways they are all alike, but they are not the same. Finding the intrinsic motivation for the organization can be a key to getting more done.

After I had been at East End Baptist Church, now 101 years old, for about two years, I met with a subcommittee of our trustees to propose getting the sanctuary of the church painted. The church had not been painted in some time, and the building, then seventy-six years old, had not been renovated in more than thirty years. Gray seemed to be the dominant color. The sanctuary walls, wainscot, and ceiling were gray. The halls, stairwells, and classrooms were gray. The vestibule, baptismal pool, and offices were . . . you guessed it—gray.

It wasn't that I disliked the color gray, but there were two things to note. For one, it was old and in desperate need of refreshing. Second, one-third of the economy of the area was military or military related. Each branch of the military has a base within an hour's drive. The area includes the largest navy base in the world, four major shipyards, and numerous other shipyards and dry-dock facilities. So that meant I had a lot of members and visitors who worked at those shipyards. And if people worked at the shipyards, guess what color they saw all day, every day? That's right, gray! And when they came to church, what color flooded their souls? Correct again: gray.

My purpose in requesting the paint job was so the members could appreciate the church and their time there in a new and refreshing way. So, as I explained my request to the trustee building and grounds committee, I just happened to throw in something like, "And I think it would be good for the kids in the church too!" I didn't know it at the time, but I had just said the *magic word*. Yes, like Groucho Marx's 1950s TV show, *You Bet Your Life*; like Aladdin's magic lamp; or even like Harry Houdini's "*Abracadabra!*" Well, not quite that easy, but close. I had stumbled onto something and didn't even know it. By the time we left that Monday night meeting, in a small upper room off the sanctuary, to request some paint for the church walls, the committee was ready to make a recommendation to the church's official board that we execute a full renovation of all of the church's facilities—all three buildings!

I came to learn that this church had a passion for next-generation ministries. From about the late 1950s to the early 1970s, this church had totally invested itself in its youth programs. Choirs, music lessons, dance troops, theatrical productions, after-school recreation, Boy Scouts and Girl Scouts, summer day camps, USDA summer food programs for kids, Ping-Pong, basketball, trips, and the list goes on. With hundreds from toddlers to teens participating, the church grew. They were criticized by many of their peer churches at the time for allowing all that "play" to happen in the church. This criticism was really jealousy because the church was leading the pack and, in this way, ahead of its time. The others did not yet realize that all the "play" was actually vibrant and transformational ministry.

All I saw when I arrived were the struggling vestiges of the former glory, and then I stumbled across the magic words, "And I think it would be good for the kids in the church too!" I soon learned that this passion for youth ministry was etched in the church's DNA. It was and remains a large part of the church's intrinsic motivation. Many of the older members have died, and many new members have come, but this passion has somehow been incorporated into the formal and informal new members' orientation and continues to be passed along from generation to generation.

Discovering and being sensitive to the intrinsic motivation of a group is a game changer. It allows the leader and the organization to begin to see things in the same light and to move forward with greater synergistic dynamism. Stating the future, change, and growth needs in alignment with the organization's intrinsic motivation may not have made the impossible possible, but it did make the possible easier. The church van was getting old. The board was not inclined to approve the needed resources until I blended the request with the church's passion for those in their formative years. Reminding them of how important this was to the growth of our youth ministry, they approved two! I could share stories of that kind over and over.

Every organization has an intrinsic motivation. For some it is as plain as the nose on your face; for others it is like trying to find a pin dropped on the other side of a crowded room in the dark. For some it is focused and stronger; for others it is more diffused and weaker. For some it is obvious. For others it may be obscure, but it is still there.

In coaching sessions with new and seasoned pastors, I have shared these insights. I challenged them to think about all they know about the group they lead, to discern their organization's inherent, underlying, core, base, fundamental, central, primary, characteristic motivation. It is asking, what is the *why* for the *what* of all they do.

- Listen to the members tell why the church is important to them.
- Hear the elders talk about the church's history and brag about their memories.
- Interview nonmembers in the neighborhood to gain their insights on the church's reputation and what they know of the benefits of having the church in the community.
- Poll the newest members and find out what drew them to the church.

This is all about recognizing that we are not all the same. What works in one place may work differently in your place. Remember, Romans 14:6 says, "Whoever observes the day, observes it for the honor of the Lord. Whoever eats, eats for the Lord, since he gives thanks to God; and whoever does not eat, it is for the Lord that he does not eat it, and he gives thanks to God."

You will get more mileage if you can align your organization's intrinsic motivation with the gospel to accomplish God's greater works. So, stop trying to be it, do it, think it, or create it in another church's image and instead do the *why* and the *what* your church and community need, as unto the Lord. This will be different for urban and rural, blue collar and white collar, resort and residential, mega and miniature, church plants and century-old churches.

➤ Leadership Study Questions ◄

1. How would you describe the community, city, or region in which your group resides?

2. How does your current community differ from the one in which you grew up?

3. What are the ministry opportunities and challenges?

4. How would you describe the people in your group demographically?

5. What are highlights of your group's history?

6. What is the intrinsic motivator for your group?

7. How can their intrinsic motivation align with the ministry opportunities and challenges?

PART 2

Vision

Begin with the end in mind.
—Stephen Covey[1]

*The only thing worse than being blind
is having sight but no vision.*
—Helen Keller[2]

*I don't believe God gives me a dream to
frustrate me.
He gives me a dream to be fulfilled.*
—John Maxwell[3]

*There are two questions that we have to ask
ourselves. The first is "Where am I going?"
and the second is "Who will go with me?"*
—Howard Thurman[4]

It must be borne in mind that the tragedy of life doesn't lie in not reaching your goal. The tragedy lies in having no goals to reach.

—Benjamin E. Mays[5]

CHAPTER 4

Get a Vision

Then Joseph had a dream.
—Genesis 37:5

It started like so many evenings. A mom and a dad at home and *their son* Jimmy playing after dinner. Mom and Dad were absorbed with jobs and did not notice the time. It was a full moon and some of the light seeped through the windows. Then, Mom glanced at the clock. "Jimmy, it's time to go to bed. Go to your room now, and I'll come see you later."

Unlike usual, Jimmy went straight upstairs to his room. An hour or so later, his mother came up to check if all was well, and to her astonishment found that her son was staring quietly out of his window at the moonlit scenery. "What are you doing, Jimmy?"

"I'm looking at the moon, Mommy."

"Well, it's time to go to bed now," said his mother.

As the boy reluctantly settled down, he said, "Mommy, you know one day I'm going to walk on the moon."

Who could have known that the boy, in whom the dream was planted that night, would survive a near fatal motorbike crash, which broke almost every bone in his body, and would bring to fruition this dream? Thirty-two years later James Irwin stepped on the moon's surface, just one of the twelve representatives of the human race to have done so.[1]

Where will you be five, ten, or twenty years from today? Where will you be in your education, your relationships, your marriage, your career, your finances, your health, your business, your church? What will you achieve between now and then? How will you know what success is and when you get there?

In my middle school glee club, I had to memorize the words to the song "The Impossible Dream,"[2] and they have inspired me ever since.

To dream the impossible dream
To fight the unbeatable foe

A dream is one of those things in life I believe everyone needs but not everyone knows how to achieve. I want to suggest today that if you want to be a success you need the *power of a vision*!

Success Begins with a Vision

Proverbs 29:18 says, "Without revelation people run wild, but one who follows divine instruction will be happy."

Whether you use the word *vision, dream,* or *revelation,* the truth is the same. When there is no vision, people perish. They cast off restraint. They live unfocused, undisciplined, unproductive lives. They stop learning, growing, and changing. They stop leading and settle for maintaining.

What goal will take you a lifetime? What are your three- to five-year goals that will help move you in that direction? Having a vision, expressed in three- to five-year goals helps keep us on track to know where we want to go and to say no to some things and yes to others.

As I reflect back over my life, I am grateful for what I believe was God-inspired vision that guided my choices. Consciously and sometimes unconsciously, a dream helped me consistently develop three- to five-year plans that have governed my steps. In middle school my goal was to go to high school. In high school it was to go to college. As a college freshman, I had a goal to graduate. The call of God changed my goal of retiring as an engineer to becoming a pastor/preacher. When starting seminary, my goal was to finish. While working as a twenty-eight-year-old pastor, my goal was to have two children in the next five years. My next five-year goal was to get a doctoral degree, then to write a book, then to get my kids through college, then to pay off my debt. All done.

People who try to live their lives and leaders who try to lead their groups without a vision find themselves settling for much less than they could achieve.

In Acts 2:17, two words talk of visions or dreams. It says, "And it will be in the last days, says God, that I will pour out my Spirit on all people; then your sons and your daughters will prophesy, your young men will see visions, and your old men will dream dreams."

Where Acts 2:17 says, "Old men will dream dreams," the word used is *enupniois*[3] from *hupnos*. It is something seen in sleep—a dream or vision in a dream.

Old men dream dreams with either hope or regret. Which one we experience when we are old depends on how we have used our years and the choices we have made. If we have acted wisely and redeemed the times, when we get old, we will have a sense of having lived a life full of satisfaction. Although we won't be here for the future, we feel we have left it in good hands, and we dream with hope of a future that will someday materialize. We have seen that our children are on the right path, and we dream with hope. We see our group, church, or business is strong, and we dream with hope. We see our nation and world have made strides in the right directions, and we dream with hope.

Isn't this what Dr. Martin Luther King Jr. said in his famous "I Have a Dream" speech. "I just want to do God's will. And He's allowed me to go up to the mountain. And I've looked over. And I've seen the Promised Land. I may not get there with you. But I want you to know tonight, that we, as a people, will get to the Promised Land. So I'm happy, tonight. I'm not worried about anything. I'm not fearing any man. Mine eyes have seen the glory of the coming of the Lord."[4]

When we have not lived life with a vision and purpose, we get old and dream with regrets of wasted days and decisions. We dream and *wish we coulda, shoulda, or woulda* done some things differently, but our energy and the beckoning eternity will not allow it.

Having a vision is essential to moving toward big results in your leadership. Look at the vision and achievement chart. The vision precedes and leads to the achievement.

Vision and Achievement Chart	
Vision	*Task to Achieve It*
An "A"	Study
Degree	Work hard to graduate
Career	Apply skills and grow
Good retirement	Save and invest
Being debt free	Discipline your spending
Being drug free	Discipline your life
Marriage	Meet your mate
Community evangelism	Share the gospel
Mature Christians	Implement discipleship strategy
You have to see it	Work to be it
You have to believe it	Work to achieve it
You have to think it	Work to do it

With Every Vision God Gives His Promise and Power to Make It True

God does not set us up for failure because ultimately His name is on the line. The testimony of His glory and His great power is at stake. Read Job 1 and see God at work. God points out Job to Satan. God removes Job's hedge of protection. God allows Satan to bring trouble to Job's life. God allows this because He is confident Job will come through the time of trouble victoriously and ultimately God's name will be praised. We see it happen in Job's life, and to this day we are reading the book of Job and praising our God Almighty!

Having a vision is about having faith. Faith that God can do what He said He can do. Faith that God will breathe on our efforts and make them successful. Here are just a few verses that remind us that God is working out His vision through the circumstances of our lives.

- I call a bird of prey from the east, a man for my purpose from a far country. Yes, I have spoken; so I will also bring it about. I have planned it; I will also do it (Isa. 46:11).
- "For I know the plans I have for you"— this is the LORD's declaration—"plans for your well-being, not for disaster, to give you a future and a hope" (Jer. 29:11).

- And God is able to make every grace
overflow to you, so that in every way,
always having everything you need, you
may excel in every good work (2 Cor.
9:8).

Don't Settle for a Plan—Get a Vision!

For the purpose of our discussion, let me say that we get into positions of leadership and know we need to do something. We come up with all kinds of plans. The organization suffers when we just run with the next new idea. It can be a good idea, but is it the right idea for this organization, at this time, in this area, and with these people? Part of the problem is that there are many good ideas. Great leaders will always have more good ideas than the capacity to execute them. Most churches do not need help coming up with something to do. If keeping busy were all there was to it, your organization might not need you. Plenty of people have an abundance of ideas about the countless activities that can be done.

Our task is not coming up with the "something." It is coming up with the "God thing." Proverbs 19:21 reminds us, "Many plans are in a person's heart, but the LORD's decree will prevail." What is the "God thing" that will move us toward the big results in His intended future?

Never settle for a plan; instead listen for God's vision.

Plan Versus Vision Assessment Chart	
It's a Plan	*It's a Vision*
If it's little	If it's almost unachievably big
If you can do it this year	If it will take you several years
If you know how to accomplish it	If you have not yet figured it out
If everybody else can see it	If only you or a few can see it
If everybody agrees with it	If some disagree with it
If you can do it by yourself	If you know the Lord has to work it out
If you can afford it	If you don't know where the resources will come from
If it takes your might	If it takes a miracle
If you decided it	If God declared it
If you get the credit	If God gets the glory!

How Do You Get a Vision from God?

Prepare Yourself

Make sure you are walking in righteousness. Don't expect God to bless you with His vision for His people if you are not in fellowship with Him.

- Read God's Word just for the purpose of hearing His voice. Sometimes we can get busy looking into God's Word, preparing for one thing or another. If you want a vision, find some time to pull away from the routine and hassle of everyday tasks. Spend some time alone with Him.

- Sing to Him and worship Him. Ephesians 4 encourages us to sing to ourselves in songs, hymns, and spiritual songs. Nothing opens the heart like singing and worshipping God, and maybe there is no more authentic worship than when we are alone.

- Confess your sins. If you are reading God's Word and worshipping Him in your heart, some light will shine on your life. If anything comes to the surface, don't deny or excuse it. Confess it!

- Submit your will to God's will. John 17 and 1 Peter 5 are great reminders that God is looking for a submitted life.

Open Your Eyes

- Look at what's going on in your leadership area. What are the strengths and weaknesses of your team? Where do they need to be ministered and where do they minister best? What training or experiences could make them more effective?

- Do a prayer walk around your community. What do you see? What needs have been left unmet? What presentation of the gospel might they best connect with?

- Look at yourself. What are your areas of giftedness and passion? Who in your group provides strength in the areas of your weakness?

Do Something

- I've seen too many leaders who have waited to do the right thing and ended up doing nothing. Sometimes God will reveal His vision to us only as we are working, not sitting.

- Find something you know you need to be doing anyway. As I initially waited for God's vision for East End, I spent a lot of my time doing visitation—homes, hospitals, nursing facilities, wherever. This was my thing, but you do something that strengthens the group and the kingdom.

- "Whatever your hands find to do, do with all your strength" (Eccles. 9:10).
- "Whatever you do, do it from the heart, as something done for the Lord and not for people" (Col. 3:23).

Ask for It

- Pray and ask. Know that God has a task for you. He would not have placed you where you are if He didn't want to accomplish through you.
- "Ask, and it will be given to you. Seek, and you will find. Knock, and the door will be opened to you. For everyone who asks receives, and the one who seeks finds, and to the one who knocks, the door will be opened" (Matt. 7:7–8).

CHAPTER 5

Cast the Vision

When he told it to his brothers, . . .
—Genesis 37:5

Joseph's father, Jacob, was blessed by the Almighty with wives, sons, and daughters. Joseph was Jacob's eleventh son, but he was the first son born to his favorite wife, Rachel. So Joseph is Jacob's favorite son, the first son of the favorite wife, and his parents made no secret that Joseph was favored. Genesis 37:3 reveals, "Now Israel loved Joseph more than his other sons because Joseph was a son born to him in his old age." But it doesn't stop there, verse 3 goes on to say "and he made a long-sleeved robe for him."

Often this verse has been translated "a robe of many colors." They even made a play about it, *Joseph and the Amazing Technicolor Dreamcoat*. Most of the children's artwork for this story shows Joseph in a rainbow-colored robe. I know, as a kid, I colored many of them myself, sometimes with horizontal strips, other times with vertical. I dressed Joseph in it on the old felt boards. I know I'm not the only one who remembers felt Sunday School boards, and Joseph had Velcro on his back so he would stick to the board. We even dressed up in the multicolored robe for a church play. The word used to describe the coat given to Joseph can be translated as either "extremities" or "diversities"[1] so the CSB reads "long-sleeved robe," where some other translations would say colors. Either way, this coat would only be worn by someone important, and that really ticked off Joseph's brothers. They hated him for his favored stature (v. 4).

Then it happened. In verses 5–11, Joseph further complicates his relationship to his brothers by telling them of two dreams he had. In both dreams Joseph was in charge and ruling the family. God had given Joseph a vision, and he shared it with his brothers.

I have to stop here to beg God for His forgiveness and confess my sin, and you might need to join me. I don't know how many times I have preached, taught, talked about, or written about Joseph and come to this point, knowing all that lies ahead for him, and thought to myself—Joseph would have been better off if he had kept his, *excuse me*, big mouth shut!

We have all heard the admonitions. Keep your dreams to yourself. You can't let everyone know your dreams because certain people out there will kill your dreams. On the contrary, there is more to what God is doing when He gives us visions that I was not considering.

Visions Must Be Articulated

I suggest that if your dream can be killed, then maybe it was just yours and not the one God has for your life or those you lead. A spiritual principle is at work here in the text, in Joseph's life, and it works in ours. Visions must be articulated!

We see it with John on Patmos in Revelation 1:9–11:

> I, John, your brother and partner in the affliction, kingdom, and endurance that are in Jesus, was on the island called Patmos because of the word of God and the testimony of Jesus. I was in the Spirit on the Lord's day, and I heard a loud voice behind me like a trumpet saying, *"Write on a scroll what you see and send it to the seven churches: Ephesus, Smyrna, Pergamum, Thyatira, Sardis, Philadelphia, and Laodicea."* (emphasis added)

We hear it in Paul and the third heaven in 2 Corinthians 12:1–5:

> Boasting is necessary. It is not profitable, but I will move on to visions and revelations of the Lord. I know a man in Christ who was caught up to the third heaven fourteen years ago. Whether he was in the body or out of

the body, I don't know; God knows. I know that this man—whether in the body or out of the body I don't know; God knows—was caught up into paradise and heard inexpressible words, which a human being is not allowed to speak. I will *boast* about this person, but not about myself, except of my weaknesses. (emphasis added)

It is a part of the lives of the Old Testament prophets like in Habakkuk 2:2:

The LORD answered me: Write down this vision; clearly inscribe it on tablets so one may *easily read it.* (emphasis added)

The old church saints might have said, "I thought I wasn't going to tell anybody, but I *couldn't keep it to myself*!

An old story is told of a woman who came forward at the invitation in a revival service and whispered in the pastor's ear that she wanted to quit smoking.

The pastor spoke loudly to the congregation, "Church, Sister Lewis just told me she wants to quit smoking!"

Sister Lewis, whispering, asked the pastor, *"Why did you tell everybody? Now I'll have to do it!"*

Ways Biblical Characters Articulated the Vision		
Receiver	Response	Revelation
Amos	Announced it	Amos 1:1–2
Samuel	Said it	1 Samuel 3:7–11
Hezekiah	Read it	2 Kings 19:14–19
Habakkuk	Made it plain	Habakkuk 2–3
David	Praised God for it	1 Chronicles 29:10–20
Isaiah	Proclaimed it	Isaiah 9:6–7
Elijah	Prophesied it	1 Kings 17:1
Jeremiah	Wore it	Jeremiah 27:1–22
Joshua	Shouted it	Joshua 6:1:21
Daniel	Interpreted it	Daniel 2:24–49
Zechariah	Admitted it	Luke 1:67–79
The wise men	Followed it	Matthew 2:12
Simeon	Sang it	Luke 2:25–32
Anna	Prayed it	Luke 2:36–38
Peter	Preached it	Acts 2:14–36
Paul	Obeyed it	Acts 26:1–29
John	Wrote it down	Revelation 1:1–11
The Lamb	Opened it up	Revelation 6:1–8:5

By Articulating the Vision

We Begin to Step Out in Faith

Why would we keep God's vision for His people secret? Most often it is because we are afraid that we will fail. You cannot do this job if you are scared. Leadership takes boldness, courage, tenacity, and faith. After all, it's not our vision; it's God's! God does not set us up for failure. It is God's name on the line anyway since it is His vision.

Let me remind you of 2 Timothy 1:7: "For God has not given us a spirit of fear, but one of power, love, and sound judgment."

If the leader does not step out on faith, how can we teach the followers to live by faith? Faith must be more than talk and a good idea. It has to be infused in the life and actions of the leader. Hebrews 11:6 speaks, "Now without faith it is impossible to please God, since the one who draws near to him must believe that he exists and that he rewards those who seek him." Did you see that? God rewards those who seek him. What better way to know we are living totally obedient to, and dependent on, God?

We Say We Are Willing to Take God at His Word

When we articulate the vision, we are announcing to the world that we are willing to take God at His Word. The sixty-six books are what I am referring to right here. God speaks through His Holy Word. Hebrews 11:1 declares, "Now faith is the reality of what is hoped for, the proof of what is not seen." Did you hear that? "Not seen!" That is exactly why it is a vision. Visions are not seen. We are trusting God's Word that says He can open doors (Rev. 3:8), that He can keep our enemies at bay (Ps. 110:1), and that He can do the impossible (Mark 10:27)!

We Give Glory to God in Advance

In Isaiah 42:8, God asserts, "I am the LORD. That is my name, and I will not give my glory to another or my praise to idols." When we are willing to announce God's vision in advance, we take away our opportunity to claim the credit and steal God's glory for ourselves.

This is amazing to me. Praising God for the not yet—not yet seen, not yet completed, not yet materialized, not yet funded, not yet supplied—is an act that stands in faith, not only on what we believe God is able to do but on what we believe God is going to do.

Giving God glory in advance frees God up to make things happen. It forces us to become totally dependent on Him, to seek His face throughout the process, and to give Him glory for each and every victory.

We Inspire Faith in Others Around Us

You cannot lead people somewhere you are unwilling to go. People are waiting and hungry to see and follow leaders who will dare to live by faith. The faith in one inspires faith in others who are witnesses. If a group is faithless, perhaps they have never seen true faith exercised in their leaders.

Those we lead learn more by what they see in our leadership than by what they hear from us.

When it comes to the practice of faith, there is no such thing as *do as I say and not as I do.* People are watching their leaders all the time, even when the leaders don't think anybody is there. They may not say it. They may never tell you what they saw, but they are always watching. Church members are hungry for spiritual leaders who will lead them to a deeper faith in Jesus.

Vision Articulation Is Preparation for Transition

Part of the importance of vision articulation, or casting the vision, is its role in preparing the group for a new future. I have repeatedly seen leaders who step into a role and almost immediately want to update the mission statement, change the structure, or do something else to reposition the organization. They feel they have to put their handprint on things right away. Maybe they have read some book or article about corporate life and believe that everything they have read applies to church life. These things may or may not apply. On the other side, I have seen pastors come to lead congregations applying the processes that worked for them in some other church experience. Again, these may or may not apply. Leading a church is not the same as leading a corporation. In a church the members you lead are also the shareholders of the organization. They are routinely vested in the life of the church in a much deeper way. Not just their time, talent, and treasure but also their family, memories, and passion. The fabric of their lives is interwoven in everything the church is. Even if the church is antiquated, off course, or in some other way broken, it is what their blood, sweat, and tears have made it.

Leaders who get into trouble in their first few years often have overlooked this vital task of vision articulation in preparation for transition. Casting the vision gets people ready for action. There is a process to change. A crisis may speed up the process, but there is a process. There are three phases to successful change. You must first change the information the church knows or has been receiving. Changing information will in time produce a change in attitude. A change in attitude is prerequisite to a change in action.

Change in Information

Both people and institutions act on available information. Leaders, through study and experience, have curated information and perspective that the institution may not possess or that the institution owns but has not assessed as relevant. Introducing new information into the church system broadens the group's capacity to respond in new ways.

Such information can, whenever possible, be introduced in comfortable ways, preferably on days you are not looking for an actual response. A passing comment in a message, "One of these days. . . ." A footnote in a presentation, "Someday we will. . . ." A portion of a prayer, "God help us to. . . ." A wish in a conversation, "It will be nice when one day. . . ." You are not asking for resources, a decision, or even a discussion. You can simply, yet strategically, cast the vision. You are the only one in the group whom needs to know you have a tactical purpose in dropping the futuristic nuggets. People cannot act on what they do not know. They can only act on what they do know. New information is always needed.

Change in Attitude

When we receive new information, over time we have to mix the new information in and cause it to make sense with all of the old data and our presuppositions. New information helps us gain a new perspective and ultimately a new attitude. Notice we still have not asked for anything except our implied desire for others to think about the new information. New information means new ideas and possibilities, which will, in time, lead to new practices.

Institutions that get stuck are societies where the rivers of new concepts have been blocked. No new concepts close the door for new creativity. No new creativity leads to stagnation and deterioration.

People have to process new criteria. It takes time for us all to uncloud our life lens and gain a new focus. A new focus must still be bounced a few times against the calcified culture of the status quo. It takes time for people's minds to break free.

Change in Action

If we patiently and persistently articulate the vision, leading our groups through the process of change will produce action.

Our church building was in the heart of one of the communities in our city. It stood tall and imposing on the same corner of the main street for more than seventy-five years in our then 113-year history. It was clear to me that we needed to move. Most of our members now came from outside the area. The neighborhood had declined some from its rich history. Our ministry was growing, but our facility was old and unable to accommodate our increasing ministry needs.

So, how do you get a 113-year-old church to move? You articulate a vision. We included in our five-year plan the limitations of our facility, the shifting demographics of our membership, and ministry we could accomplish with an updated facility. *This was new information.*

We did not call it a "church" in this plan. We called it by its real name, a "facility." If we did not learn any other lessons from the coronavirus quarantine of 2020, I hope we learned this: The church building is not the church. Our church buildings were closed for a period of time, but the church was never closed. The church *is* the people of God. The building is merely a facility whose sole purpose is to facilitate the ministry of the church.

By continually talking about new ministry possibilities a facility update could bring us, it was not long before the members were willing to agree, without a single dissenting vote, to the Nehemiah and Moses plans.

Both Nehemiah and Moses are great biblical models for moving organizations forward. Our challenge must always be to prayerfully determine which *kairotic* moment we are in. Chronological time is the time on the clock or calendar, but *kairotic* time is different. *Kairotic* time is a time when conditions are right for the accomplishment of a crucial action: the opportune and decisive moment. We cannot rush it or calendar it, but we must be ready to act in it.

Nehemiah renovated and built up the walls around Jerusalem. Moses led the people to the Promised Land. So the Nehemiah Plan was for us to stay where we were, renovate, and add on to the facility. The Moses plan was to find a new piece of land, build a new facility in the new location, and move. We agreed that we would give every effort to try to sensibly execute the Nehemiah plan, but if we could not, we would automatically switch to the Moses plan.

We put the vision for the new facility in our five-year plan. It took six years to find and secure the right property for the new ministry campus. It was ten years from the initial vision to finalize our building plans. Since the old facility was not in a growing, high construction area, its sale was a challenge. As we put it on the market, we planted seeds casting visions with several pastors who had smaller facilities or were farther out in the rural area and might want to move into the city. It took ten years for these seeds to grow. Yes, it was ten years from the time we put our old facility on the market until it sold. Six years were necessary to raise the cash we needed through our capital campaign. It was thirteen years from the vision until we finally got all needed city permits and approvals. The seventeenth year brought a great celebration as the construction and move were finally completed.

Everything can't be rushed. Casting the vision gives time for people to embrace the new ideas, plans, and directions. Things need to move according to God's time.

CHAPTER 6

Wait for It

They hated him even more.
—Genesis 37:5

About two months after I started at the East End
Church, I remember riding somewhere with one of
the church trustees. In our conversation as we rode
along, I mentioned I had a lot of ideas about things we could
do and what needed to change at the church. This older
seasoned gentleman counseled me, saying that if I had some
ideas about the church, I should tell them now so that everyone would know. I responded by saying, "Not yet." I was not
sure if these were God's visions or just my ideas. Running
too quickly with our own ideas has gotten many leaders into
trouble, and it is the reason some do not last long in their
positions. We will address longevity later, but for now, just
know God has a vision for you and those you lead, but you
may have to wait for it.

This may be the hardest thing about visions—the wait.
Waiting speaks to a time that is not now. In this age of the

Internet, we have become accustomed to getting things right away. We feel online purchases should be delivered the next day; we should be able to cook any meal in thirty minutes; people should answer texts within seconds. We forget that sometimes we must wait.

Remember Ecclesiastes 3:1 and 11, "There is an occasion for everything, and a time for every activity under heaven. . . . He has made everything appropriate in its time." If everything is appropriate in its time, then the same things can be inappropriate out of their time. You don't withdraw from your 401k retirement account at age forty. If you do, there is a penalty because the withdrawal has taken place at an inappropriate time. You don't drive through an intersection when your light is red. You don't greet your future spouse on the first meeting with a romantic hug and kiss. You don't get off the passenger jet while at thirty thousand feet in the air. However, if you wait to withdraw from your 401k till you are the right age, there is no penalty. If you wait for the green light, there is no accident. If you wait until you're dating, you are not seen as a lecherous creep. If you wait till the jet lands, you are still alive at the end of the flight. Why? Because you allowed the actions to take place at the appropriate times.

Habakkuk 2:2–3 heralds this word: "The LORD answered me: Write down this vision; clearly inscribe it on tablets so one may easily read it. For the vision is yet for the appointed time; it testifies about the end and will not lie. Though it delays, wait for it, since it will certainly come and not be late." There are at least three important things for us to see in these verses about visions. First, when God gives you a vision for the group you lead, write it to remember it. Second, trust where the vision is taking you. It is not showing you now; it is showing you then. Third, wait for it. Be patient. Do not step ahead of God because you may end up doing your thing instead of God's thing.

A Vision Will Take You Places You Were Not Anticipating

I had a recent conversation with a pastor in my hometown of Philadelphia, Pennsylvania. We met years ago as teenagers in summer camp. He marveled over my having moved to Louisville, Kentucky, then to Suffolk, Virginia, and now to Nashville, Tennessee, over the years of my ministry career. My response was that none of these moves was a part of my plan. I made each of these moves only in response to a specific call of God. Taking a line from the late comedian W. C. Fields, "All things considered, I'd rather be in Philadelphia." Even more than that, though, I want to be in the place of God's appointment.

Most of us would like Genesis 37:5 to say, "Then Joseph had a dream. When he told it to his brothers . . . , and, like Chef Emeril Lagasse, "BAM!" the vision came to fruition." Instead, it ends in an unexpected and unappreciated way: "They hated him even more."

Some, in commenting on this part of Joseph's life, have criticized him. Joseph has, I believe, been falsely accused of self-promotion and arrogance. Joseph faithfully worked with the sheep. He was the favored son through no fault of his own. He did not ask for the long-sleeved ornate coat that, by its design, shouted, "This man is a leader!" He did not lie, twist, shade, or exaggerate about the images God gave him. He simply was who he was and did what God wanted him to do.

Is the pastor wrong to preach the truth of the gospel? Is the leader wrong to declare, "This is what the Word of God says!"? The answer is obviously no. There are times when the Word of God makes people uncomfortable or even mad, but that is no reason not to preach it, teach it, or be led by it. But let's say Joseph didn't tell his dreams. Let's imagine that Joseph never said a mumbling word about the visions God had given to him and kept them to himself.

If Joseph had never told the visions, his brothers would not have plotted to kill him. He would not have been thrown into a well, sold into slavery, or taken to a foreign country. He would not have been sold to Potiphar, an officer of Pharaoh and the captain of the guards. He would not have done so well on his job that Potiphar would leave town and leave Joseph in charge, thus giving Mrs. Potiphar the opportunity to falsely accuse him of rape.

If Joseph had never told the visions, he would not have been thrown into an Egyptian prison where he would not have had the confidence to interpret the dreams of the

Pharaoh's baker and the cupbearer, be forgotten by those he helped, remembered years later, and called on to interpret Pharaoh's dreams. He would not have had the opportunity to share a plan to save Egypt from the coming famine and thus be elevated to serve Pharaoh. If he were not in place to serve Pharaoh in the famine, he could not have saved Israel.

Even Joseph, himself, looks backwards over the experience in Genesis 45:5 and 50:19–20 and sees God's guiding hand and providential plan.

> "And now don't be grieved or angry with yourselves for selling me here, because God sent me ahead of you to preserve life." (Gen. 45:5)

> But Joseph said to them, "Don't be afraid. Am I in the place of God? You planned evil against me; God planned it for good to bring about the present result—the survival of many people." (Gen. 50:19–20)

Remember, we only see the horizon. A vision does not give every detail about the future. God knows if we knew everything we were going to go through to get where God wants us, many of us would quit before we even started. Some would give up long before the end. Some would be too bitter, angry, resentful, and unforgiving over what they knew to be useful. What kept Joseph going despite the hardships was a vision! The path was not the one he selected.

It takes time to see and then time to accomplish a vision. Wait for it.

A Vision Will Cost You Something

The road was long. Joseph was seventeen years old when his brothers threw him into the pit (Gen. 37:2). He was thirty years old when he first entered Pharaoh's service in the palace (Gen. 41:46). So it was thirteen years from the pit to the time Joseph first enters the palace. Jewish tradition suggested Joseph may have spent twelve of those years in prison.[1] If we add on the seven years of the plentiful harvest, then from the vision to the fulfillment was at least twenty years, and thirteen of the twenty were hard years.

A young preacher was in the process of making some bad decisions for his life and ministry. He exclaimed, "But God wants me to be happy!"

The seasoned pastor questioned him: "Was Noah happy building a huge boat in a place where no one could even conceive of the idea of a flood? Was Abraham happy when God told him to leave his home and business and walk around Canaan for the remainder of his life? Was Moses happy as he spent forty years in the wilderness with a constantly complaining crowd? Was Joshua happy fighting thirty-one kings after having walked around the walls of Jericho until they fell down? Was Job happy to be stricken by grief and sickness? Was Daniel happy in the lion's den? Were Shadrach, Meshach, and Abednego happy in the fiery furnace? Was

Peter happy under persecution? Was Paul happy in prison? Was John happy in exile on Patmos? Was Joseph happy to be sold into slavery? And was Jesus happy to be crucified on the cross?"

> Then he said to them all, "If anyone wants to follow after me, let him deny himself, take up his cross daily, and follow me. For whoever wants to save his life will lose it, but whoever loses his life because of me will save it." (Luke 9:23–24)

> "If anyone comes to me and does not hate his own father and mother, wife and children, brothers and sisters—yes, and even his own life—he cannot be my disciple." (Luke 14:26)

God does not call us to be happy, comfortable, rich, or popular. The call to follow Jesus as a disciple is the call to sacrifice. It is the only way to accomplish the vision.

A Vision Will Keep You on the Path to Success!

When I get in the car, I almost always turn on my GPS. Work commute or cross-country, I use my GPS. Why? It sees things down the road that I can't see. It helps me avoid traffic slowdowns, speed traps, detours, accidents, tolls, and more. If you are like me, sometimes my GPS tells me to make a turn, and I miss it. Sometimes the turn was not obvious, my GPS told me too late, the turn came up too fast, or I was in the wrong lane. What I love is that the GPS doesn't get frustrated or upset. It keeps its focus on the destination, the vision, and reroutes me so I can get back on track moving forward to the goal.

The movie *Flight of the Phoenix*, original 1965, remake 2002, based on a true story chronicled in the 1964 novel *The Flight of the Phoenix* by Elleston Trevor, is about a group of people who survive an aircraft crash in the Gobi Desert and must build a new aircraft out of the old one to escape. With limited water and supplies, lost in the desert, one of the crew feels the vision of rebuilding the aircraft is pointless. He determines he will walk out of the desert to safety. The captain warns him not to make such an attempt. He questions why. The captain tells him without the ability to focus on a goal in the distance he would think he was walking in a straight line but would actually be walking in circles. The captain continues instructing, telling the young man everyone's legs are uneven. One is ever so slightly shorter than the other, and without knowing it we will make a shorter gait on one side and walk in circles in a desert until we die.

Isn't this what is happening to many leaders and groups? They end up walking, working, living, existing in circles, never getting any closer to a goal.

A clarified vision helps us know we are making forward progress. It keeps us on track and lets us know when we have reached our desired and intended destination.

Hebrews 12:1–2 says,

> Therefore, since we also have such a large cloud of witnesses surrounding us, let us lay aside every hindrance and the sin that so easily ensnares us. Let us run with endurance the race that lies before us, keeping our eyes on Jesus, the pioneer and perfecter of our faith. For the joy that lay before him, he endured the cross, despising the shame, and sat down at the right hand of the throne of God.

Just as fixing our eyes on Jesus moves us toward success in the Christian life, keeping our eyes on the vision guides us as we move ever closer to our goal.

➤ Leadership Vision Questions ◄

1. What is God's vision for your group?

2. How does it differ from what your group is already doing?

3. What new information will help your group begin to see the need for change?

4. What are the challenges you already know you will face as you move toward making the vision a reality?

5. Are there difficulties you can avoid as you move toward making the vision a reality?

PART 3

Execute

Without strategy, execution is aimless.
Without execution, strategy is useless.
—Morris Chang, CEO, Taiwan
Semiconductor Manufacturing[1]

It's easy to dream about it . . . much
harder to execute it . . . work!
—Gary Vaynerchuk[2]

The method of the enterprising is to
plan with audacity and execute with vigor.
—Christian Nestell Bovee[3]

God will perfectly position us
to execute his plan.
—Leah DiPascal[4]

*But if it doesn't please you to worship
the* LORD, *choose for yourselves today:
Which will you worship—the gods your
ancestors worshiped beyond the Euphrates
River or the gods of the Amorites in whose
land you are living? As for me and my
family, we will worship the* LORD.
—Joshua 24:15

CHAPTER 7

Make a Decision

Then the king asked me, "What is your
request?" So I prayed to the God of the
heavens and answered the king, "If it
pleases the king, and if your servant has
found favor with you, send me to Judah
and to the city where my ancestors are
buried, so that I may rebuild it."
—Nehemiah 2:4–5

Not every vision takes a long time to materialize. Not every vision has to come into enough focus so you can know what you have to do, at least to make the first steps. Joseph had dreams of sheaves and stars and over time had to figure out what those would mean for his life. Not so for Nehemiah. Nehemiah received a report about the condition of his homeland, specifically Jerusalem. Nehemiah 1:3 says, "They said to me, 'The remnant in the province, who survived the exile, are in great trouble and disgrace. Jerusalem's wall has been broken down, and its gates have been burned.'"

This news struck Nehemiah hard. He sat, wept, mourned, fasted, and prayed. We don't know exactly how long Nehemiah prayed. He prayed that God would, and believed He should, do something about the condition of the city and the distress of the people living there. In his prayer he reminded God of God's greatness, His promises, His people, and the investments He had already made in them.

As Nehemiah prays, one thing becomes clear: he himself is God's answer to his own prayers. The words in the end of Nehemiah 1:11 seem to jump out of nowhere and seem utterly disjointed from the remaining text of Nehemiah's prayer. He concludes by saying, "At the time, I was the king's cupbearer."

"I was the king's cupbearer!" Living in Susa, the capitol city, and being paid well, maybe he had a chariot equivalent to today's Tesla and was living in a home that would rival the designs of Chip and Joanna Gaines. As swiftly as Hurricane Laura passed through Lake Charles, Louisiana, in 2020, Nehemiah's vision cleared like bright blue skies when the storm is gone.

It dawned on Nehemiah that he worked for the king. He was the *king's* cupbearer. He ate whatever the king ate. He drank what the king drank. He lived in the place where the king lived. He had the complete trust and confidence of the king. Nehemiah had great prestige, prominence, and power. Nehemiah not only kept unwanted food from the king, but he kept away unwelcomed foes, folly, and fortune hunters. Here's the point: God never gives us an experience just so we can say we've been there. God never gives us resources just so we can say we have them. God never puts us in a position just so we can be proud. God places each of us in strategic settings so we can meet the right people, say the right word, or influence the right path.

Once we have clarified God's vision, it is time for action. Action never begins without a decision to get up, to take up, to walk up, to speak up. When we get to chapter 2, we find Nehemiah in the presence of the king on a normal day, serving in his usual role, but something unusual happens. The king asks Nehemiah a question, "What is your request?" and Nehemiah had an answer.

A dream or goal can be pursued and achieved in many ways, but you will never complete a task without making a decision to start on one of them. Some people are crippled by indecision.

On a hot summer day, a little boy was given two delicious ice popsicles. One ruby red cherry and the other green goblin apple. They both melted in his hands, and he never got to taste either one. Why? He couldn't decide which one he wanted to eat first. Indecision will keep a batter from hitting a home run, an investor from benefiting from a big increase, and you from realizing your God-implanted dreams.

When the big opportunity arrived and the king asked the question, "What is your request?" Nehemiah had an answer. He did not hesitate or hem and haw. His vision from God did not come in a dream, and it was not for some far-off time. It was something that needed immediate attention. It was a vision for a man of action, and Nehemiah was ready!

Nehemiah 2:5 reports, "If it pleases the king, and if your servant has found favor with you, send me to Judah and to the city where my ancestors are buried, so that I may rebuild it." It is one thing to have a vision of what should be done. It is another to make a decision to actually do it.

When I first started preaching in Philadelphia, my pastor was leading a group of churches that were about to do evangelistic tent revivals for eight consecutive weeks in a new location of the city each week. It was a big deal. It took a lot of planning, resources, coordination, city approvals, workers, publicity, training, and more. We had to clean abandoned lots, move and pitch a massive tent with lights, instruments, chairs, and more. It was an exhausting yet rewarding summer, to say the least. A little before the actual crusade began, the group had invited a pastor from another city to preach during the big kick-off event. This all happened many years ago, but that preacher's words still ring in my ears. Encouraging the gathering, he declared, "We, for a long time, have just been talking about something like this, but you are doing it!"

People meet and meet and talk and talk. Some have one dream or good idea after another, but nobody celebrates the planners, talkers, dreamers, thinkers, or pontificators. We celebrate the deciders and the courageous doers! I loved it when George W. Bush described the job of the president of the United States of America as the "decider in chief." Nothing will ever get done in the absence of a decision.

Making a decision is part of the challenge. Making the right decision is the other. We all have some expertise in making bad choices, but what does the leader need to keep in mind to make good ones? The five things a leader must weigh are the times, trends, talents, direction, and destination.

Times

We previously discussed that the difference between the times of Moses and Nehemiah was the scope of a task. Now we must also discern the difference between a Joseph and a Nehemiah time when it comes to the timing of our decisions. Had Joseph acted on his vision when he received it at age seventeen, he would have been a failure. The times were not yet right. Not only was Joseph not in the right location, position, and maturity, but the season of famine, that pulled everything together, had not yet arrived.

For Nehemiah the scenario was totally different. Nehemiah was in the right location, position, and maturity; and the season of destruction, that pulled everything together, had arrived. Whether it's dancing, driving, dieting, dating, dreaming, or deciding, the times can make all the difference. In Isaiah 60:22 the Lord says, "The least will become a thousand, the smallest a mighty nation. I am the

Lord; I will accomplish it quickly in its time." Don't ignore those last three powerful words—*in its time!*

We love Ecclesiastes 3:1, "There is an occasion for everything, and a time for every activity under heaven" and 3:11, "He has made everything appropriate in its time," until they apply to us, our circumstances, and what we want. Sometimes we want to wait when God says, "Go," and other times we want to go when God says, "Wait."

Timing may be why I never got the hang of Double Dutch. In my birth order I am sandwiched between two sisters. So that meant sometimes I would end up playing their games. One such game was Double Dutch. Jumping two sets of ropes that formed intersecting circles or ellipses at the same time. There is one timing for jumping a single rope. A totally different timing for jumping Double Dutch. Needless to say, I never gained the skill of jumping Double Dutch, or maybe subconsciously I never wanted to so I would not have to participate.

Discern God's time and be faithful to it. God may give you a burning passion like Nehemiah. God might put obstacles in your path like Joseph. God may have circumstances closing in on you so you have no other choice like Moses at the Red Sea. You never know when or where His timing will present itself. Sometimes I have found it in personal devotional reading of God's Word. Other times in the counsel of others spiritual people close to me. I'm sorry that there is no one or easy answer to this one, but finding God's timing is key.

Trends

By trends we are trying to answer the question, How do we minister in the contemporaneous context? This is recurrently not the place where the teams we lead reside. Leaders influence forward momentum and transition. Groups tend to settle in places of familiarity and comfort. Consequently, groups do many things out of routine, habit, and tradition. This can be a good thing until these things get out of sync with the society we serve. Then they may be good things to do, but they no longer meet the prime objective impacting those outside the group. Without the infusion of a true leader, groups over time are disposed to become self-serving societies wholly out of touch with the times and trends of the day.

Airbnb manages relationships making it possible for homeowners to rent their properties to strangers. Through Airbnb, travelers can pick the location, dates, and type of dwelling they want to stay in. Owners make their vacation or primary domicile available. The travelers get the convenience and comfort of staying in a home rather than a hotel and often in prime locations. Owners get opportune marketing solutions and extra cash. Airbnb started in August 2008. By 2017, according to *Business Insider*,[1] they had more listings worldwide than the top five hotel brands put together.

Netflix was a new company that began an Internet-based DVD-by-mail subscription service in the late 1990s. Netflix grew and expanded. In 2000, the owners made an offer to Blockbuster, the leading store-based VHS and DVD rental company, to sell Netflix for $50 million. An article in *Inc. Magazine* is titled "Blockbuster Could Have Bought Netflix for $50 Million, but the CEO Thought It Was a Joke: John Antioco's arrogance in September 2000 cost Blockbuster its future."[2] Blockbuster filed for bankruptcy in 2010 and closed its last store in 2013. According to *Forbes*, as of April 2020, Netflix was worth $194 billion.[3]

Why is it that some succeed while others fail? Businesses, churches, and organizations frequently fail for a common cause. Do you remember Borders, Blockbuster, and Compaq Computers? They all have the same story. They were at the top of their game, but they all failed to see the trends and innovate toward them. They have all gone out of business.

Many church leaders read Matthew 16:18, "And I also say to you that you are Peter, and on this rock I will build my church, and the gates of Hades will not overpower it." However, they make the mistake of concluding that they and their church cannot fail. Not true. This verse is Jesus talking about His church, the universal church of all the saints of all the ages. This is not a promise for any local church. Local churches do fail. They do close. How we respond and adapt to trends matters. The gospel never changes, but how we minister it to each generation must accommodate the current trends.

Getting groups to see and adjust toward the trends can be problematic when they are tightly tied to the traditions and historical elements of the past. These bring a sense of comfort. Sometimes in situations like this, you have to help people look back to move forward. Help them see why or how they developed those traditions in the first place. Make a connection with the timeless that helps them focus on the current trends. Then use that remembrance to encourage them to join the change to do it again.

Every church in decline had a great day. My one-hundred-year-old church that was showing clear signs of deterioration had theirs in the 1960s. In the 1950s, they had renovated the facility, and by the 1960s the church was at its peak. The music, the ministry, the methods, and more propelled them to become *a*, if not *the*, leading church in the community. Major city influencers were a part of the congregation, and hundreds of teenagers participated in their youth ministry—after school and weekend recreation, summer day camps, choirs, dramatic acting productions, and more. The youth ministry became a special source of pride for the congregants.

One of the problems with success is our desire to hold on to it. Leaders intuitively act on the notion that the best way to hold on to success is to keep things as they are. They believe they have found the formula for which everyone has been searching through the ages. So they work to maintain and keep everything just as it was when it brought them great success. What they don't realize is that the only real way to hold on to success is to adapt to the new trends and create new achievements.

They were at the top of their game in 1960. Unfortunately, when I came almost thirty years later, they still believed it.

Since they believed it, they were still doing everything just as they did in the early 1960s. The facility was still the same, the music was still the same, the worship was still the same. The leaders where largely still the same except those who had been replaced because of death. The church believed it was still the same. So much so, that when I would go to the youth ministry meetings, the kids would be talking about the hundreds of teens who were participating in the church's youth ministry. I looked in bewilderment. The room was empty. There weren't enough teens to fill one table! What I came to grasp was that the teens' parents had told the old stories of the glory days of their youth so many times that even the parents' kids, who had never seen any of the years of success, believed it was still happening.

If nobody observes trends, you will surely die. The leader has to have eyes open to see what is really happening in the church, in the community, and in the world. Once seeing, the leader has to be the catalyst ready to stimulate the organization toward a new future. The leader must be like the Issacharites. First Chronicles 12:32 declares, "From the Issacharites, who understood the times and knew what Israel should do."

Talents

Members of the group will often come to the leader with ideas about what ought to be done next. Sometimes these propositions can be helpful and insightful and other times not. One thing that helps the leader decide is the talent in the group. There are two vital diagnostic questions concerning talents when trying to determine what to do next.

The first question is, What talents are available in the group? We can do what we can do, and we cannot do what we cannot do. I firmly believe that one way God lets us know what we ought to be focusing on next is by the talents that are available. God places the talents in the body to fulfill the mission and ministry He has designed for your church. Over the years there have been great ideas I've had or that were brought to me, but at that moment we did not possess the talents to realize it. Sometimes this means this is not for you. Sometimes this will mean this is not for you right now.

There are three basic ways to get talent in your congregation.

1. **Teach/learn the skill.** This takes time, but it deepens your group's capacity as several persons develop the needed skill set.

2. **Hire the skill.** If you can bring financial and talent resources together, this is a viable option. However, sometimes you don't have the money to hire a skill and even if you did, you must also determine whether this is the right long-term strategy to employ in this area.

3. **You can pray for the skill.** Never under-
   estimate the power and purpose of
   prayer in these situations. This is God's
   work, and prayer is a vital ingredient.
   Sometimes during our time of prayer,
   God is also putting some other things
   in place so that when He answers we
   are actually carrying out His task in His
   timing.

The second question is, Are the talents in the group
ready to be used? Do not discount this question.

1. **The probable leaders we need may not
   have capacity at the moment.** They may
   already be wearing too many hats at
   church, at home, at work, and in the
   community, but there may be a foresee-
   able time when some things will come
   off their plate so they can be devoted to
   the new task.

2. **The potential leaders may not be loyal.**
   This should not be overlooked! Do these
   leaders trust your leadership, and are
   they willing to follow? Every person you
   work with does not have to love you,
   or even like you, but they do need to
   have a love for the future viability of the

organization, a respect for you as the leader, and a willingness to follow.

3. **The plausible leaders may not be spiritually ready.** Maybe they have the right skill but are young Christians in need of a little more spiritual maturity. Maybe they are members who have been around for a while but have glaring moral issues that have been left unaddressed. Why reward the wrong set of behaviors? The rest of the members are watching, and they will emulate the behaviors you reward.

Be careful; don't fix one problem and at the same time create a bigger one. This is God's work. Trust His timing.

Direction

Some leaders only look inward at what is already going on so they can improve it. But at some point this becomes something like rearranging the deck chairs on the *Titanic*. Some only look outward at what others are doing so they can bring it to their location, but this approach alone may duplicate ministry that is already happening in the community or bring activity that may not work in your local context.

Look outward to see what is not happening in your community. What are the needs being left unserved? Find the void where no church or group is stepping up and stepping in. This is admittedly harder for some leaders, but this is where having an entrepreneurial instinct really pays off. It may be helpful to talk to different types of people in the church, the community, the surrounding businesses, and the government.

When Walmart, McDonalds, or Starbucks opens a store, they have already done community and market research so they know that with the right management their franchise can thrive. For success in business, they say location, location, location. Church life is a little different. In the past we have often just looked for an available building or piece of land; and if you are at an older church, your location has been chosen for you a long time ago. Understanding the lives and needs of the people in your church field is still germane. Some denominations offer their churches a ministry mosaic of their church field or maybe go to your chamber of commerce, visitor's bureau, or planning department.

Whatever you do, don't be a "Hound-Dog Leader." In the old days, when a farmer was riding to town, he would be on a wagon with a horse, and his hound dog would run up front. The problem was the hound dog never could figure out the way to town by himself. He would run up front as if he were leading the way until they came to a fork in the road. Since the hound dog did not know the way, he would sit at the fork unable to decide which way to go. The old horse knew the way, and even without prodding from the farmer, at the fork of the road, the horse would make the right choice. After the horse had chosen, turned, and passed the fork in the road, the hound dog would get up and run back in front of the horse as if he had been leading all the time.

Don't pretend to be the leader—lead! Do your research, walk in prayer, have faith, but do not paralyze the church through fear and indecision. You will not always get everything right, but even then, trust Romans 8:28, "We know that all things work together for the good of those who love God, who are called according to his purpose."

Destination

It is always amazing to me to talk about movement and destination with an institution that is not changing location. The local church is as much an organism as it is an organization. Organisms must be nourished. They grow, expand, and mature; and if they are not revitalized, they die. You must indeed move your organization toward a destination. Visions, goals, and dreams keep an organization alive! They help provide purpose and meaning for its existence. They are reminders of why the members ought to work, stay, plan, and give.

When the church is stuck in an old time, you must cast a vision of a new future and a new destination. In addition to all we have already discussed, the words of an old hymn, "A Charge to Keep I Have,"[4] helped remind me of my mission, especially verse 2:

A charge to keep I have,
A God to glorify,
A never-dying soul to save,
And fit it for the sky.

To serve the present age,
My calling to fulfill:
Oh, may it all my pow'rs engage
To do my Master's will!

Arm me with jealous care,
As in Thy sight to live;
And O Thy servant, Lord, prepare
A strict account to give!

Help me to watch and pray,
And on Thyself rely,
Assured, if I my trust betray,
I shall forever die.

It was written by Charles Wesley in 1762 and based on Leviticus 8:35, "You must remain at the entrance to the tent of meeting day and night for seven days and keep the LORD's charge so that you will not die, for this is what I was commanded."

It is an old song, but it is a continual reminder that our task is unceasing to this current age. What others did in their time may have been great and appropriate for then but not for now. Each year brings a new dawning of a new age. New days, opportunities, and challenges require new ideas, methods, and ministry. Churches fail when we serve the past age. We are only relevant when we serve this present age. My son in his twenties once asked me, "Dad, how was this back in your day?"

My response was, "Son, my day is still going on." Never stop changing, growing, learning, and adapting, and God will never stop using you for His glory.

CHAPTER 8

Make Progress

So we rebuilt the wall until the entire wall
was joined together up to half its height, for
the people had the will to keep working.
—Nehemiah 4:6

I n 1983, the Westfield Sydney to Melbourne Ultramarathon[1] was established. The winner would receive a $10,000 prize. The race was a distance of 544 miles from Westfield Parramatta in Sydney to Westfield Doncaster in Melbourne, Australia. It was about like running from Miami, Florida, to Columbus, Georgia; New York City to Lancing, Michigan; Los Angeles, California, to Albuquerque, New Mexico; or Paris, France, to Pisa, Italy.

The world's greatest distance runners gathered for the event. They were mostly in their twenties, young and fit, and dressed in the latest Nike, Puma, and Adidas shorts and running gear.

Unexpectedly a sixty-one-year-old potato farmer also showed up. He arrived dressed in overall jeans, gum boots, and a baseball cap. His name was Albert Ernest Clifford Young, but most people just called him Cliff.[2]

They asked Cliff questions like, "Have you ever run in a race?"

Cliff responded, "No. I just thought I want to."

"What makes you think you can even finish?" they inquired.

Cliff replied, "We have two thousand sheep on two thousand acres of land. When I have to corral the sheep sometimes, I have to run two to three days without even sleeping."

As the race began, the world-class runners all started out at a good pace. Their plan was to run eighteen hours and sleep for six hours each day. But nobody told Cliff Young there was a strategy.

Cliff ran at a slow loping pace that later became known as the Cliff Young Shuffle. He trailed the leaders for the first day, but by running while the others slept, he took the lead the first night and maintained it for the remainder of the race, eventually winning by ten hours.

The Westfield Sydney to Melbourne Ultramarathon took Cliff five days, fifteen hours, and four minutes, almost two days faster than the previous record for any run between Sydney and Melbourne. A number of future ultra-marathon runners adopted what became known as the Cliff Young Shuffle. Several that adopted this strategy won the ultramarathon.

This was the old tortoise-and-hare story come to life. Cliff became somewhat of a folk hero, so much so that another six-day marathon was established and named the *Cliff Young Australian Six-Day Race.*

That sixty-one-year-old potato farmer knew one of the keys to success in any endeavor. If you have a winning strategy, stick to it.

Abraham knew this. In Deuteronomy 11:24, God told him, "Every place the sole of your foot treads will be yours. Your territory will extend from the wilderness to Lebanon and from the Euphrates River to the Mediterranean Sea."

So, what did Abraham do for the remainder of his life? Well, he never bought a house, that's what! Instead he lived in tents. He kept moving from place to place, and by doing so, he enlarged the territory that would become the inheritance of his generations. Success is rarely without a struggle and almost always with a strategy.

Paul, the apostle, gave his life for the advancement of the gospel of Jesus Christ. He traveled long rocky roads, sailed tempest-tossed seas, spoke to unfriendly crowds, and faced adversarial leaders. In his own words, he said,

> "On frequent journeys, I faced dangers from rivers, dangers from robbers, dangers from my own people, dangers from Gentiles, dangers in the city, dangers in the wilderness, dangers at sea, and dangers among false brothers; toil and hardship, many sleepless

nights, hunger and thirst, often without food, cold, and without clothing." (2 Cor. 11:26–27)

When we get to the fourth chapter of Nehemiah, he gives a progress report. Nehemiah tells what has been done: "So we rebuilt the wall until the entire wall was joined together up to half its height" (v. 6). He goes on to tell how he was able to make this achievement: "for the people had the will to keep working." Here, we will unfold the things that are essential for progress: people, patterns, and practices.

People

No significant work is ever accomplished by a lone individual. "No man is an island entire of itself; every man is a piece of the continent, a part of the main," says John Donne in his poem.[3] This excerpt from *Meditation 17* is one of a series of poems he wrote when he was seriously ill in the winter of 1623.

On March 22, 1964, in a speech in Saint Louis, Missouri, Dr. Martin Luther King Jr. said, "We must learn to live together as brothers or perish together as fools."[4] We could also note Barbra Streisand's signature song in the 1964 Broadway musical *Funny Girl*: "People, People who need people, Are the luckiest people in the world."[5]

It's been said a number of different ways: leadership is the ability to influence others to do great things. So, if you are doing everything, you are not a leader. Instead, you are only a doer. You cannot be a leader in isolation or in a vacuum. It takes people.

Nehemiah understood this. He knew there was no way for him to take on the enormous task of rebuilding the walls of Jerusalem by himself. He knew more things get done when individuals work together rather than alone.

Five important qualities a leader needs to work with and through people are encapsulated in these five words: *credibility*, *course*, *communication*, *credit*, and *chirk up*.

Credibility

Credibility is the trustworthiness of an individual. It is a quality that allows people to have faith, confidence, and belief in the leader and the leader's vision. Nehemiah came from the king's palace with letters of authority and a core team. Nehemiah 2:9 says, "I went to the governors of the region west of the Euphrates and gave them the king's letters. The king had also sent officers of the infantry and cavalry with me."

Credibility is not a specific title or position. If you have to tell people you are in charge, you probably lack credibility.

Nehemiah was not called director of the King's Jerusalem Revitalization Project, or something like that. Instead, it was clear he had found success, even in exile, that gave him credibility. His personal Jerusalem connections and genuine passion for the city and its people gave him leverage.

A title is great, but credibility is greater!

Course

People don't just buy into you; they must also buy into where you want to take them—your course, your plan, your vision. This also means that in some way you must be able to share it. People can't subscribe to what they don't know, hence the articulation of the vision. Nehemiah shares his course in 2:10: he "had come to pursue the prosperity of the Israelites."

Note that Nehemiah was noble and unselfish. He was not there to enrich himself or do his friends a favor. He wanted to benefit those who were struggling. People can support your leadership when it is moving on a course toward an acceptable shared future. It needs to be a win-win.

Communication

Nehemiah understood he had to get the message out. It was not enough for the information just to be in the leadership team.

> So I said to them, "You see the trouble we are in. Jerusalem lies in ruins and its gates have been burned. Come, let's rebuild Jerusalem's wall, so that we will no longer be a disgrace." I told them how the gracious

hand of my God had been on me, and what the king had said to me.

They said, "Let's start rebuilding," and their hands were strengthened to do this good work. (Neh. 2:17–18)

Did you hear the end of verse 18? "And their hands were strengthened to do this *good* work!" (emphasis added). That is what happens throughout chapter 3. The people are doing the work.

- Priest (v. 1)
- Men (v. 2)
- Sons (v. 3)
- Supervisors (v. 5)
- Goldsmith and perfume maker (v. 8)
- Daughters (v. 12)
- Inhabitants (v. 13)
- Rulers (v. 14)
- Levites (choir members) (v. 17)
- Priests from the surrounding region (v. 22)
- Temple servants (church staff) (v. 26)
- Guards (v. 29)
- Merchants (v. 32)

There was only one group that did not join in the effort. They are revealed in verse 5. It says, "Beside them the Tekoites made repairs, but their nobles did not lift a finger to help their supervisors" (Neh. 3:5). Yes, the nobles did not lift a finger! Do not wait for 100-percent participation or support. You will never get it. Love all. Communicate to all. Go with those who can see the value of the work.

Credit

Though men have quoted, misquoted, and put their own spin on this saying, in 1863, a Jesuit priest named Father Strickland is quoted as saying, "One may do a great deal of good in this world if one does not care who gets the credit for it."[6] I guess the fact that so many others have taken or been given credit for the quote is a tribute to the quote itself. A friend with his own twist on this often says, "I don't care who gets the credit as long as God gets the glory."

Leaders who do not understand leadership will sometimes try to hog the credit and dominate the spotlight. They don't realize that the leader always gets the credit . . . and the blame. It comes with the job. There is no benefit in trying to steal the small spotlight someone else on the team may get from time to time. Let others have their day. Let them bask in their fifteen minutes.

Giving and sharing the credit makes people willing to work longer and harder. Nehemiah understood this, and so he is able to report in chapter 4, "So we rebuilt the wall until the entire wall was joined together up to half its height, for the people had the will to keep working" (v. 6). No credit hogging here. Nehemiah gives it all away. Now think for a minute. Whose name is on the book? Who is the only person whose name all of us remember from this story? There is only one: the leader's name—Nehemiah. As long as you are working hard doing your job, when it comes to credit, the more you give, the more you get.

Chirk Up

People's enthusiasm for any tasks will ebb and flow. It will share both high moments and low. Do not get overconfident in the highs or overly depressed in the lows. Do not live in the extremes, but know they both come and go. As the leader, you help people celebrate the highs. They may be so engaged in the work that they don't notice that something wonderful, extraordinary, or special just happened unless you bring it to their attention. You also help your team navigate the lows. Perspective makes all the difference. Down in the valley, I may not notice the sun is shining brightly. If I am on a path I have never traveled, I may not know that my goal is right around the bend. In both situations, *chirk them up!*

In all honesty, I had never heard of this phrase until I was looking for a nice "C" word that communicated the idea of encouragement. This one does. To *chirk up*[7] is "to fill with courage or strength of purpose." Opposition was rising against Nehemiah and the work, and so he chirks up the team in Nehemiah 4:14:

> After I made an inspection, I stood up and
> said to the nobles, the officials, and the rest

> of the people, "Don't be afraid of them. Remember the great and awe-inspiring Lord, and fight for your countrymen, your sons and daughters, your wives and homes."

Since the leader sees what the people can't see, the people feed off of whatever the leader is providing. "Follow the Leader" is much more than a child's game. It is a truth of life. If the leader is courageous, the people are courageous. If the leader is loving, the people are loving. If the leader encourages unity, the people hold ranks and encourage unity. But if the leader is fearful, hateful, or otherwise discouraged, the people will also follow the leader there.

Chirk up your church, your team, your family, your marriage, your children, your community. Maybe this is why David reminded us in Psalm 118:24, "This is the day the LORD has made; let's rejoice and be glad in it!"

Practices

Sustained progress requires the implementation of practices that promote long-term win-win solutions for both the leader and the group being led, a true partnership.

We see this recommended and exemplified by Jesus in Matthew 20:25–28:

> Jesus called them over and said, "You know that the rulers of the Gentiles lord it over them, and those in high positions act as

tyrants over them. It must not be like that among you. On the contrary, whoever wants to become great among you must be your servant, and whoever wants to be first among you must be your slave; just as the Son of Man did not come to be served, but to serve, and to give his life as a ransom for many."

Paul, the apostle, commends this practice in Philippians 1:3–5.

I give thanks to my God for every remembrance of you, always praying with joy for all of you in my every prayer, because of your partnership in the gospel from the first day until now.

Even King David illustrates practices that promote long-term win-win solutions. In 2 Samuel 9:1, David asked, "Is there anyone remaining from the family of Saul I can show kindness to for Jonathan's sake?" Saul is at this point dead. David has ascended to the throne. Customarily, a king might kill or banish all of the family members of his predecessor. Instead, David seeks to show kindness.

Had Rehoboam been more inclined to do something similar like listening to the counsel of the elders, Israel might not have become a divided kingdom. We see Rehoboam's bad example in 1 Kings 12:6–8.

Then King Rehoboam consulted with the elders who had served his father Solomon when he was alive, asking, "How do you advise me to respond to this people?"

They replied, "Today if you will be a servant to this people and serve them, and if you respond to them by speaking kind words to them, they will be your servants forever."

But he rejected the advice of the elders who had advised him and consulted with the young men who had grown up with him and attended him.

Nehemiah, in chapter 5, presses home the need for servant leaders to practice social justice and advocacy on behalf of the people they lead.

Leaders Need to Practice Compassion

Progress can bring internal problems. Here the people were devoting so much time, energy, and resources to building the wall that they likely had left the harvest of their own fields to understaff teams. The wage earners and landowners were struggling, and the children were becoming slaves to pay off the family debts. With the pressure on, the people were mounting to get the tasks done. Nehemiah was not a predator but had compassion for the people. Nehemiah 5:6 says, "I became extremely angry when I heard their outcry and these complaints."

People want leaders and want to follow those leaders, but the leaders need to exhibit empathy and compassion.

Leaders Must Practice Championing the Causes of Others

Nehemiah became a champion for the people, not an adversary. Sometimes the people served will need a champion to speak up for them. Nehemiah not only spoke up for the people, asking for relief for the suffering people, but he also did his best with the resources available to him to rectify the situation. Nehemiah 5:8–10 continues:

> "We have done our best to buy back our Jewish countrymen who were sold to foreigners, but now you sell your own countrymen, and we have to buy them back." They remained silent and could not say a word. Then I said, "What you are doing isn't right. Shouldn't you walk in the fear of our God and not invite the reproach of our foreign enemies? Even I, as well as my brothers and my servants, have been lending them money and grain. Please, let's stop charging this interest."

Some leaders seek to enrich themselves at times at the expense of others. Remember this: a rising tide lifts all boats. Ecclesiastes 11:1 (CEV) says, "Be generous, and someday you will be rewarded."

I always love the fact that in Matthew 25, as Jesus describes the great separation and final judgement, those working for God never realized it.

> "Then they too will answer, 'Lord, when did we see you hungry, or thirsty, or a stranger, or without clothes, or sick, or in prison, and not help you?'
>
> "Then he will answer them, 'Truly I tell you, whatever you did not do for one of the least of these, you did not do for me.'"
> (vv. 44–45)

These champions were not looking for a reward. They were trying to do what was right. And in doing what was right, they inherited an eternal reward.

Leaders Should Comfort Those They Lead

Nehemiah understood that he was to be a comfort and not a burden to the people he served. In verse 15, he notes that the previous governors had heavily burdened the people, but Nehemiah chose instead to be a comfort to the people. Nehemiah 5:18 describes it this way:

> Each day, one ox, six choice sheep, and some fowl were prepared for me. An abundance of all kinds of wine was provided every ten days. But I didn't demand the food allotted to the governor, because the burden on the people was so heavy.

This is much like the qualifications for leaders in the New Testament, recorded in 1 Timothy 3:2: "An overseer, therefore, must be above reproach, the husband of one wife, self-controlled, sensible, respectable, hospitable, able to teach." We also see this in Romans 12:13: "Share with the saints in their needs; pursue hospitality."

Patterns

"You're so random!" is what we would say when a person starts talking about a disconnected thought that seemed to come out of nowhere. Just as a random comment can be confusing and even frustrating, so is leading at random. While consulting with a pastor of a large church, I said, "This church is like an eighteen-wheeler fully loaded, racing down the highway, but you are driving it like it's a motorcycle weaving in and out of traffic." You get the idea. The weight, size, and momentum of a fully loaded eighteen-wheel truck will not allow it to weave in and out of traffic like a motorcycle can. We non-motorcycle riders feel this bobbing and weaving on the highway to be a bit reckless, but for a Mack Truck, the collateral damage would be horrific.

Coming up with a design for the future of your organization is one thing. Sticking to it and getting it to completion is another. When you are passionate about the group's future and can see the ministry potential, you can get idea after idea, dream after dream. The problem is that it is easy to design a future that has more things happening than you have the capacity to execute.

So, what do we do with our abundance of futuristic plans? Again, differentiate which are God's plans for you, your group, and this time. Remember this: "Many plans are in a person's heart, but the LORD's decree will prevail" (Prov. 19:21). Commanding a sea of selections, seizing a plethora of possibilities, is both normal and nice. I'd rather have to pick from a surfeit of great plans than to die in a famine of fresh ideas.

The struggle of many leaders, including me during those early years, is sticking with a plan to its completion. We see this in people all the time. Every year many make some New Year's resolutions. Here are the things we are going to do or change, start or stop, get or give up this year. But many resolvers forget all about their dreams by the end of the first quarter. In fact, clinical psychologist Joseph Luciani reports, just 8 percent of people attain their New Year's objectives, while about 80 percent fail to hang on to their New Year's resolutions.[8]

This problem with sticking to the objective is not unique to our annual resolutions. It is a greater issue of commitment and execution. This is why God's Word encourages us in Proverbs 16:3, "Commit your activities to the LORD, and your plans will be established."

Sean Covey, Jim Huling, and Chris McChesney, in *The Four Disciplines of Execution*, give four key strategies that help us clarify the plan and follow it to completion.[9]

- Discipline 1: *Focus on the Wildly Important.* Less is more! We often focus on too much at one time, more than we have capacity to execute. Choose only the most impactful two or three goals at a time.
- Discipline 2: *Act on the Lead Measures.* Find some things you can influence that will lead to the achievement of the goal. Don't just measure the goal. Measure the things you are doing consistently that lead to the goal.
- Discipline 3: *Keep a Compelling Scoreboard.* People play harder when you are keeping score. A scoreboard helps the group to know whether they are winning or losing so they can refine their strategies and focus their efforts to achieve the goals.
- Discipline 4: *Create a Cadence of Accountability.* Out of sight, out of mind, as the old saying goes. The team needs to be held accountable for each week's efforts that will lead to the triumphant attainment of the goals.

These four items seem simple, but they frequently go missing as many of us seek to concentrate our efforts on completing the designed future state.

An additional helpful tool is found in Gary Keller's *One Thing: The Surprising Truth behind Extraordinary Results.* He discusses *goal setting to the now.*[10] The basic idea it that we need to do something to move us toward the achievement of our goals every day. This works as a great complement to the *Four Disciplines of Execution.* To put it simply, look at each of your two to three WIGs (Wildly Important Goals) and break them down in bite-sized chunks. Let's say you have a five-year goal: What do you need to accomplish this year to make sure you achieve the five-year goal? Once I know what I have to achieve this year, I ask, "What do I need to complete this month? To succeed this month what do I need to attain this week? Knowing what I need to complete this week, what then must I finish today?" This is a great strategy to keep us on track and make every day count as we make progress toward our longer term goals.

CHAPTER 9

Make Friends, Make Enemies

*When Sanballat, Tobiah, Geshem the
Arab, and the rest of our enemies heard
that I had rebuilt the wall and that no gap
was left in it—though at that time I had
not installed the doors in the city gates—
Sanballat and Geshem sent me a message:
"Come, let's meet together in the villages
of the Ono Valley." They were planning
to harm me. So I sent messengers to them,
saying, "I am doing important work and
cannot come down. Why should the work
cease while I leave it and go down to you?"*
—Nehemiah 6:1–3

About two months after arriving at East End Baptist
Church, I recall riding in a car with one of the senior
church leaders. Since I was only twenty-eight, he

was easily old enough to have been my father. Naturally, we chatted as we rode, exploring our still new relationship. I was wondering who this guy really was, and he, I'm sure, was wondering the same about me. We conversed about our personal community and even national history, and everything was great! Then we started talking about the future. I remember saying something like, "I have a lot of thoughts about what we can do with the church moving forward."

"Stop." The tenor of the conversation changed. With his back now straight, brow now furrowed, tone now stern, he asked, "What are these plans? You better let us know before we get too far down this road."

I knew the road he was referring to was not the one we were driving on but the one I was dreaming on. I responded, "Not yet, these thoughts are not ready to be heard." By this I meant two things. One, that I was not sure if these were just my ambitious thoughts or God's ambitious vision. They are not the same. Sometimes leaders rush off to carry out their thoughts without checking to see if they are also God's vision. But second, and maybe just as critical, we did not yet have the strength of relationship needed for that conversation.

Friends

Whether you are the pastor of a church, the president of a club, or the CEO of a Fortune 500 corporation, you need friends. If you want to make significant moves, big changes, or faith leaps with an organization, you need friends. You have to have strong relationships with those you lead so they will be willing to make the jump with you.

Dr. Gary Chapman in his excellent work *The 5 Love Languages* reveals the five ways we all give and receive love: words of affirmation, acts of service, receiving gifts, quality time, and physical touch.[1] He also talks about our love tank and suggests that we must work to keep the love tank of the one we are in a relationship with full. The kinds of acts of love the other receives helps to fill up and maintain the fullness of the other's love tank. Making a big change or mistake is more easily accepted if the love tank is full, but results can be tragic if the love tank is empty.

This concept of "filling the love tank" applies in leadership scenarios as well. I have too often seen leaders, totally new to an organization, make big directional, missional, philosophical, or even physical moves in the first months of their tenure. Most times they do not succeed, and they either cripple their ability to make needed changes in the future or even lose their position completely. The whole issue here is making friends, or in Gary Chapman's terms, filling up the love tank.

So, other than cake, coffee, and conversation, how do you make friends in and with an organization?

Acknowledge

Even if things aren't as you believe they should be, know that the members of that organization worked to make it whatever it is. They are invested. Appreciate the work and sacrifices of the past. Even though a new day has dawned, those sacrifices were good for the past. Let them know that you want to be as courageous and faithful in your stewardship of this time as those before were in theirs.

Ask a Lot of Questions

Don't assume you know everything. Questions communicate that you are interested in them, in what they have achieved, and where they think they want to go. Ask *what*, but also ask *why*. Sometimes you may not understand why they do something, but when they give you their rationale, it may make perfect sense. Other times when you ask why, they may be without an answer, and that opens the door for you to suggest a better way.

Achieve a Win!

Not something you want but something they want. Find something your organization has been wanting or trying to accomplish for some time and do it. Make it happen. This invariably creates friends. It puts something in the tank so you can make a withdrawal when you are ready.

Accompany

There is no substitute for spending time with people, especially in their space. Meetings are good; meals are better. Homes, hospitals, and local hangouts all afford ways to get to relate, know, and see people in a more personal light and for them to see you as well.

Enemies

We all like making friends, but if you are going to move an organization forward, you must be willing to make enemies. If you are not making somebody uncomfortable, you probably are not doing your job. The key is not making everybody mad at the same time.

A person can become an enemy for a number of reasons, even if you do everything right. Jealousy, envy, control, power, money, change, and comfort all lead to experiencing someone as an adversary. Things were going fairly well for Nehemiah, but in chapter 6 his opponents try to make a full-frontal attack. They mean Nehemiah harm and not good.

Jesus had only loved, healed, fed, and helped people, yet His detractors crucified Him on a cross. Hear Jesus in Matthew 10:34–38:

> Don't assume that I came to bring peace on
> the earth. I did not come to bring peace, but
> a sword. For I came to turn
>
> > a man against his father,
> > a daughter against her mother,
> > a daughter-in-law against her
> > mother-in-law;
> > and a man's enemies will be
> > the members of his household.

> The one who loves a father or mother more than me is not worthy of me; the one who loves a son or daughter more than me is not worthy of me. And whoever doesn't take up his cross and follow me is not worthy of me.

Jesus was not saying He wants us to be mean, nasty, or obstinate and make people hate us. He was simply warning us that we will not be able to stand against sin or move organizations forward without someone becoming antagonistic. So know this tough thought. When it comes to leadership, especially in the church, here's a Crostonism: You can't do your job if you are not willing to lose your job! Or better yet, Jesus said it this way in Matthew 16:25: "For whoever wants to save his life will lose it, but whoever loses his life because of me will find it."

A momentary caution: sometimes, as with Nehemiah, our enemies are truly against the work of the kingdom, but there are times when our "enemies" are there to help us see the error of our own ways. Use the old quote from an unknown source to help you discern which is which.

> Don't mind criticism.
> If it is untrue, disregard it;
> if unfair, keep from irritation;
> if it is ignorant, smile;
> if it is justified, it is not criticism;
> learn from it.[2]
> —Anonymous

Focus on the Value of the Work

That is exactly what Nehemiah did. Though he was approached and attacked by foes repeatedly, he understood his greater cause. He knew his efforts were not for personal gain but for the glory and the purposes of Almighty God. He spoke as much to himself as to the enemies who were calling him to meet his destruction. "So I sent messengers to them, saying, 'I am doing important work and cannot come down. Why should the work cease while I leave it and go down to you?" (Neh. 6:3).

Charles Schwab once said, "I have yet to find the man, however exalted his station, who did not do better work and put forth greater effort under a spirit of approval than under a spirit of criticism."[3]

Forgive Sinful Folly

Sometimes your enemies are your enemies. Sometimes they are opponents of the project, and sometimes they are their own adversaries. Yes, that's right! The resistance you meet at times will have nothing to do with you or the project. We all encounter broken, hurting people who pour their personal pain on others. They do it habitually; they don't even realize it. Hurt people really do hurt people. So be wise as serpents and harmless as doves.

Did you realize that all you need is one "r" to turn *fiends* into *friends*? The "r" that a fiend needs is the one in *reconciliation*. If you are thin-skinned or hold grudges, take that to

God in prayer. You cannot be a successful part of the healing ministry if you yourself hold on to hurt. Second Corinthians 5:18–19 informs us,

> Everything is from God, who has reconciled us to himself through Christ and has given us the ministry of reconciliation. That is, in Christ, God was reconciling the world to himself, not counting their trespasses against them, and he has committed the message of reconciliation to us.

As in the experience of every leader, when I went to East End, everyone had not voted for me, and everyone was not in love with me. Some were indifferent, and some had postured themselves as adversaries. Rather than sulk or complain, I stood firm in my convictions, never stopping efforts to love and care for them. They loved the church, too. They just had a different vision for its future. I can honestly say that somewhere during those twenty-six years, all my enemies had become not only friends but were also my greatest supports, and others even became like family. One "r" does make a difference. Always be ready for reconciliation.

Fixate on the Future

If you preoccupy your mind with the patterns of the past or the problems of the present, those patterns and problems may overtake you. You will not win every contest. Sometimes you must strategically lose a battle so you can win the war. It may sound counterintuitive, but it is true. Losing gracefully on a nonessential element can be part of spiritual shock and awe. It serves to let others know that you are really on the team and it is not just all about you and your way. In a war every battle is not worth winning.

Judge Paul Pressler shared in his book *A Hill on Which to Die,*

> In any great movement are individuals who sit back and watch to see which way the battle will go. When they see which side will prevail, they attach themselves to that side. These people disturb me, because they seem to be self-serving individuals who are more interested in their own advancement than they are in basic principles. They are more concerned with their own future than they are with the cause itself.[4]

Keep your eyes on the prize. Rather than fixate on every pattern or problem, sustain your focus on the future and keep persistently advancing. Forward is not always a straight line. It is most often a meandering path.

Fortify Your Testimony

We cannot achieve God's purposes via Machiavellian politics, where the end justifies the means, or by Malcom X's politics, *by any means necessary.* Romans 6:1–2 demands, "What should we say then? Should we continue in sin so that grace may multiply? Absolutely not! How can we who died to sin still live in it?"

We can only accomplish God's goals in ways that will bring God glory. Nehemiah was aware of this as he refused to join Sanballat and Geshem in the villages of the Ono Valley. We can never stoop to the level of our provocateurs. As leaders we must live in such a way that even if people made up an evil report against us, no one would believe it.

➤ Leadership Execution Questions ◄

1. What are the most important decisions you need to make?

2. What are your two to three Wildly Important Goals?

3. What needs to happen for you to make significant progress?

4. Who is not onboard? What are their underlying issues? How can you minister to them? What are their open criticisms? What can you learn from them?

5. What is the most important goal you have for the next five years? This year? This month? This week? Today?

PART 4

Team

Talent wins games,
but teamwork and intelligence
win championships.
—Michael Jordan[1]

If you want to lift yourself up,
lift up someone else.
—Booker T. Washington

No one can whistle a symphony.
It takes a whole orchestra to play it.
—H. E. Luccock

Coming together is a beginning, staying
together is progress,
and working together is success.
—Henry Ford

*The way a team plays as a whole
determines its success. You may have
the greatest bunch of individual stars in
the world, but if they don't play together,
the club won't be worth a dime.*
—Babe Ruth

*What's true for a teammate
is also true for the leader:
If you don't grow, you gotta go.*
—John C. Maxwell[2]

*Two are better than one
because they have a good
reward for their efforts.*
—Ecclesiastes 4:9

CHAPTER 10

Build a Team

As he passed alongside the Sea of Galilee,
he saw Simon and Andrew, Simon's
brother, casting a net into the sea—for
they were fishermen. **"Follow me," Jesus**
told them, "and I will make you fish for
people." *Immediately they left their nets*
and followed him. Going on a little farther,
he saw James the son of Zebedee and his
brother John in a boat putting their nets in
order. Immediately **he called them,** *and*
they left their father Zebedee in the boat
with the hired men and followed him.
—Mark 1:16–20, emphasis added

Because I grew up, went to college, and had my first postcollege career in Philadelphia, Pennsylvania, I am all things Philadelphia even though I have not lived there for many years. Philadelphia has a reputation for having the most honest fans, who love to give immediate feedback on whether their teams are doing a good job. We have not had many championships over the years, but we have had some. One notable championship was Super Bowl LII, on February 4, 2018. The most famous play was dubbed "The Philly Special," sometimes also called "The Philly Philly." It was a trick play at the end of the second quarter where quarterback Nick Foles, at the last-minute, steps out of the QB position. Running back Corey Clement steps into the QB slot. Immediately after the snap, he makes a backwards pass to tight end Trey Burton. Trey Burton makes a pass, and Nick Foles becomes the receiver to score a touchdown. I do not know how many times I have watched this play. The Eagles won over the New England Patriots, 41 to 33. As good as they are, neither the Eagles' Nick Foles nor the New England Patriots' quarterback, Tom Brady, could have won by themselves. In the end it was not who had the better players but who made the better team.

Know the Importance of Building a Team

At the beginning of his public ministry, one of the first things Jesus does is build a team. All of the Synoptic Gospels report it—Matthew 4:18–22; Luke 5:1–11; and Mark 1:16–34. Jesus is *the Son of God, Savior of the world, miracle working Messiah, King of kings, and Lord of lords*, yet His first act is to put His team in place.

Here, Jesus practices an axiomatic principle of leadership, and that is, *you are not a leader if you don't have a team to lead.* Six significant dynamics happen when leaders and teams get together.

Compounding

There is a limit to how much one person can accomplish. Studies have shown how many man-hours it takes to accomplish certain tasks, and recommendations are made on the data. Teams help us multiply our efforts. I can only be in one place at a time, but a dispersed team can be in several. I can only lift two hundred pounds, but the team and I can lift a ton. Leaders limit their impact by trying to do everything themselves. Leaders compound and multiply their achievements by empowering their team. One Savior can die on a cross, but a team of apostles can take the message to the ends of the earth.

Contribution

Every member of the team brings a requisite skill. None of us possesses every talent the team needs to be effective. If you are a jack-of-all-trades, you will be the master of none. The apostle Paul emphasizes this in 1 Corinthians 12:12–27 and Romans 12:3–8 about team church. Romans 12:4–5 says, "Now as we have many parts in one body, and all the parts do not have the same function, in the same way we who are many are one body in Christ and individually members of one another." In a well-functioning team, every team member makes a unique contribution, and every role is necessary for the team's success. This is not static. There will be times when the current team's configuration no longer works, and persons, assignments, and/or positions need to change to maximize contribution again.

Cooperation

People can be good at their task, but they may not be good in the area of cooperation. When a quarterback calls the play, skilled players who are determined to run their own routes decrease the effectiveness of the team. Skillful players who are antagonistic, contrary, independent, and dogmatic hurt team morale. They stifle team collaboration, creativity, and keep the team from peaking at its potential. A team must have synergistic cooperation to be its most effective.

Dr. J. V. Bottoms Sr., who served many years ago as pastor of the Green Street Baptist Church in Louisville, Kentucky, had several short but powerful sayings to live by. One of them was, "It is easier to operate when we cooperate." A team that cooperates always accomplishes more. Except for Judas Iscariot, the disciples were willing to prove over and over again that they were on the team through their cooperation.

Collective Purpose

This is the idea of going in the same direction or reaching for the same goal. It is the achievement of the collective purpose that brings teams together. All effective teams have one. The collective purpose may be set in a number of ways, but once determined, it serves as a driving force. In a team looking for big results, all team members, whatever their role, agree on the team's collective purpose.

Ants may not look like it, but they are organized and are working toward the colony's collective purpose. They are organized in a caste system with a queen, males, and workers. The queen lays eggs, the males have sex, and the workers dig the tunnels, clean the eggs, gather food, and care for the young. In fulfilling their collective purpose, they also help in our collective purpose. As ants dig tunnels, they aerate the soil. As they take seeds deep in the earth to feed the colony, they are disbursing the seeds. And once underground, many of the seeds sprout before the ants can eat them, and instead the seeds form new plants.[1]

Jesus' invitation for fisherman and others to join His team included His purpose and what would be their collective purpose. "Follow me," he said in Mark 1:17. And then came the purpose: "I will make you fish for people."

Cohesion

One of the great blessings of being part of a real team is cohesion. This comes because the teams have spent time together in various milieus, at the task, at the table, during off times, and over a period of time. They learn about one another's particularities, passions, pasts, prospective, potential, and penchants. They become more than just coworkers. Their hearts and lives are invested in one another. They come to respect one another. Their futures, successes, and even failures are intertwined. Their relationship that starts as a loose tie can move to a Velcro-like grip and even to a superglue bond.

Anyone who has been a part of a viable team knows and appreciates this. Teams stick together. Jesus' disciples faced great difficulties during His life, at His crucifixion, and after His resurrection, but they were by this time a team, and they stayed together.

Create times for the people you are building into a team to share times and experiences away from the main tasks. Go to lunch, dinner, a ball game, a retreat, or a mission project together. Take a genuine interest in them; talk about life, family, and their future. Remember birthdays, anniversaries, kids, and challenges. Be encouraging. Avoid sarcasm and gossip. Show up at family funerals for support. All of these help create team cohesion.

Chisel

We should make teams better, and teams should make us better. No member is yet what they will become. Build your team by looking at and for potential.

Potential is that which is in something or someone that is not yet revealed, matured, or used up.

- In a seed there is the potential for a forest.
- In a fish there is the potential for a school.

- In a bird there is the potential for a flock.
- In a cow there is the potential for a herd.
- In a girl there is the potential for a matriarch.
- In a boy there is the potential for a patriarch.

You may not always see potential on the surface, but you must always believe it exists. God delights in our potential. David was a boy; God saw a king. Amos was a shepherd; God saw a prophet. Moses was a murderer; God saw a leader.

Jesus chose real people—imperfect souls, individuals with room to grow—as His disciples.

- Matthew was a tax collector. Need I say more?
- James and John were selfishly ambitious.
- Peter was a cussing, sword-carrying fisherman.
- Judas was a backstabber.
- Simon was a fanatical zealot.
- Thomas was a doubter.
- Bartholomew asked Philip, "Can anything good come out of Nazareth?" (John 1:46).
- James son of Alphaeus, is totally obscure. He did nothing noteworthy by any of the Gospel writers.

- Thaddeus wanted Jesus to take a more public stand.
- Phillip was so focused on the physical, at the feeding of the five thousand, he failed to see the spiritual answer sitting in front of him.
- Andrew was a follower.

Jesus did not require His disciples to have everything right. Instead, "Calling the crowd along with his disciples, he said to them, 'If anyone wants to follow after me, let him deny himself, take up his cross, and follow me'" (Mark 8:34).

Jesus knew the one task of the leader is to chisel the team. Not to leave them as they are but to make them better. Proverbs 27:17 says, "Iron sharpens iron, and one person sharpens another."

Jesus taught them. He illustrated and demonstrated for them. He sent them out to try and sometimes fail. He gave them honest, helpful evaluations. He repeated this process over and over to help them learn and find confidence. He invested three years in His disciples before He told them in the Gospel of John that He had to go away. By then they had been thoroughly chiseled. Over time Jesus took that motley crew and developed them into a team to whom He could entrust the life and development of the church, the teaching of His Word, and the spread of the gospel throughout the world.

Now Go Get the Players

So, where can you find your dream team? You could conclude that Jesus found His walking along the water so we all ought to spend more time at the beach. While this sounds good to me, let's look again and dig a little deeper. What else do we know about the disciples? They were all already busy doing something. One was busy collecting taxes. Some were occupied catching fish. One was great at networking, bringing others onboard. And one was deep into the politics of the day. Even Judas must have had some skill that qualified him to become the group's treasurer!

What people are doing gives us some indication of their skill set, passion, and work ethic. The disciples were from a variety of occupations and walks of life, but none were just sitting around and waiting for something good to come their way. Remember the man at the pool of Bethesda in John 5? He waited thirty-eight years for an angel to trouble the waters and someone to put him in at the right time. Jesus healed him but never asked him to join His team. Why? Maybe there were thirty-eight years' worth of waiting reasons.

It has been said, *if you want to get something done, ask a busy person.* Jesus found and called people who were already busy and occupied. What do I see in this? Don't be limited to those who are already doing what you need them to do. All of Jesus' disciples changed careers to follow Him. Don't be limited to those others think are the right mix for your team. The stigma of lying and cheating that surrounded Matthew's profession would have disqualified him in many people's eyes. And yet Jesus called him. Don't be intimidated by the passion of people; learn to channel it. Others probably thought Simon the Zealot would be too wild and opinionated for the team, but Jesus called him.

In 1 Samuel 16, Samuel went to Jesse's house in Bethlehem because God was ready to change His team leader. Saul had failed in 1 Samuel 13, and God sent Samuel to anoint a new king. Samuel looked at Jesse's oldest son and immediately concluded that he was the man for the job. God let Samuel know the oldest was not the right choice, so Samuel looked at the next, then the next, and then the next until it appeared that none were left. God told Samuel in verse 7, and we must remember this too, "Do not look at his appearance or his stature because I have rejected him. Humans do not see what the LORD sees, for humans see what is visible, but the LORD sees the heart."

We must prayerfully ask God to help us see more than their present but also their possibilities and potential. After all, where were you, what were you doing, who were your connections, and how was your life when God called you into His service?

Note, ultimately it is God who chooses, and He always chooses for a purpose. He makes this plain in John 15:16:

> "You did not choose me, but I chose you. I
> appointed you to go and produce fruit and

that your fruit should remain, so that whatever you ask the Father in my name, he will
give you."

I remember being interviewed by the pulpit search committee of a church. They asked me something like, "Are you
willing to accept this call if we choose you?" My answer was,
"Likely yes, but remember this choosing goes two ways. As
you are choosing me, I am praying, asking God if He wants
me to choose you."

We also see this in 1 Samuel 16:1:

The LORD said to Samuel, "How long are
you going to mourn for Saul, since I have
rejected him as king over Israel? Fill your
horn with oil and go. I am sending you to
Jesse of Bethlehem because I have selected
for myself a king from his sons."

I know people like to sing songs that say, "I kept on
searching till I found Him," but truly, God was never lost
and is still the prime mover unmoved. God completed the
plans of salvation before the foundations of the world were
laid. He chose us before we had the ability to even think
about choosing Him.

This ought to bless somebody. Maybe there was a time
when you weren't picked for a team, a job, the prom, a marriage, a scholarship, a school, a position, a promotion, or a
church. Just know that while they were not selecting you,

God had already chosen you. He has already chosen to love you, to save you, and to use you for His glory and His eternal purpose. Yes, God always chooses with a purpose: "I have selected for myself a king from his sons" (1 Sam. 16:1).

We don't always select with a purpose, but God does. I can remember going on vacation one year when my children were small. We packed everything we needed for my wife, two small children, and myself into a tiny Chevy Nova, and off we went. At some point on our way, we stopped at a BJ's Wholesale Club, maybe to get milk for the baby, and my wife saw a comforter set. She had to have it. I tried to dissuade her, reminding her we did not have any room to spare in the tiny Nova and that we could pick one up after vacation when we returned home. She was not hearing any of what I was saying. She had to have that comforter set. So, you know what I did? That's right! I bought it. Why? Because we were on our way for a week's vacation; and, like the old saying goes, if momma isn't happy, nobody's happy. And I wanted to be happy on our week of vacation. We moved and pried and found a way to get that comforter into the already fully packed car and went on our way.

After our wonderful week away, we returned to our home and unpacked the car. Do you know where we put the bed comforter set that we had to have before we went on vacation and packed into the tiny Nova? We put it in the closet! And do you know how long the pretty bed comforter sat in the closet? Years! Until one day, seeing it in the closet,

I yanked it out and threw it on one of the beds, determined that we were actually going to get some use out of it.

Well, my wife was not the only one like that. I am sure some reading this right now have some things in their houses they had to have but have never used—some shoes, some tools, some dishes, some clothes. God never does that. When God picks, He always picks with a purpose in mind.

God has a purpose for each of our lives and for every member of our team. It is important that we find and actualize God's purpose for our lives.

If I were picking a football team, I would not pick haphazardly or just because you were my friend. (Sorry, I like to win.) Friendship is great! We all need friends in our personal lives, but *friend* and *function* are two different words. This is a notice we can and will have people on our teams whom we do not always like personally. Even if we don't want to invite the person home for dinner, this should not prevent us from having a cordial working relationship on the team.

So I would pick someone who could throw with accuracy to be my quarterback, someone solid yet agile to serve as center, and someone who was fast with good catching hands to be my wide receiver. You get the idea. Each player has a particular purpose, and the purpose is in the mind of the leader. Gather the team with the potential and skills you need to gain your big results.

CHAPTER 11

Set the Standard

*But you should **select** from all the people*
able men, God-fearing, trustworthy, and
*hating dishonest profit. Place **[Set]** them*
over the people as commanders of thousands,
*hundreds, fifties, and tens. They **should***
judge the people at all times. Then they can
bring you every major case but judge every
minor case themselves. In this way you will
lighten your load, and they will bear it with
you. If you do this, and God so directs you,
you will be able to endure, and also all these
*people will be able to go home **satisfied**.*
—Exodus 18:21–23, emphasis added

If you aim at nothing you will hit it every time."[1] I am not
sure if this is Zig Ziglar's most famous quote, but it certainly is to me. Setting the standard is all about giving
your team something to aim for. Anecdotally, what I have
seen over the years is that when there is no clear standard

for the team, they acquiesce to the strongest personality. This could be great if it is a personality that wants to move in the right direction, allows others to express themselves, and encourages others to grow in their own leadership skills. Unfortunately, leaving things up to the chance of the strongest personality being all those things may not get you where you want to go. It typically makes the members of your team settle at being followers rather than growing in their leadership qualities.

Many organizations never reach their potential. Many frustrated leaders conclude that the people God gave them to work with just cannot or will not do any better. The frequent truth, however, is a clear and achievable standard has not been given.

In Exodus 18, Moses is trying to be a one-man show. He is *doing* instead of *leading*. Remember, if you are *doing* everything, you are not a *leader*; you are just a *doer*. Moses' father-in-law, Jethro, recognizes this problem and gives Moses some helpful guidance to set a new standard for the leaders and the leadership processes. Let me pull out the four verbs in Exodus 18:21–23 that make this happen. They are *select, place, should,* and *satisfied*. Technically, *should* is an auxiliary verb and *satisfied* is an adjective, but you get the point.

To set a standard you must *select* leaders. Jesus selected the twelve disciples, and Moses was instructed to select his group of leaders. Not every volunteer will do. There always needs to be a standard for those who will lead. Notice they are to be:

1. from all the people,
2. able,
3. God-fearing,
4. trustworthy,
5. and hating dishonest profit.

You can find books written on each one of these, so I will not elaborate on them extensively here. These criteria are formidable by themselves. These are the minimum entry norms.

From All the People

Leaders should never be selected if they are not from the people. Volunteers should be from the membership of the church. Staff should be from the members of the denomination and doctrine.

Able

Chosen leaders should have the ability or acumen for the task. They need, at least, the potential to grow in and with the position so the organization can succeed.

God-Fearing

Many secular, carnal, or immoral people have mastered skills that could be useful in the kingdom of God, but if they are not committed to the King, they are not the right fit for the job.

Trustworthy

When it comes to relationships, organizations, or even governments, trust is certainly part of the glue that holds them together.

Hating Dishonest Profit

This does not just say honest or not greedy, but more emphatically for our American capitalist culture, it pushes farther to say "hating." First Timothy 6:10 declares it:

> For the love of money is a root of all kinds of evil, and by craving it, some have wandered away from the faith and pierced themselves with many griefs.

To set a standard you must *set* leaders. Each leader must be in the position to complement others and maximize their contributions. Exodus 18:21 reminds us that all leaders are limited, not just by their giftedness but also by their capacity. Some who are good at leading hundreds will, in time, increase their capacity and later can govern thousands, but some will be great at leading fifty, and that really is their sweet spot. Ten might be too few and to many hundreds could hinder leaders from maximizing their personality and talents for the tasks at hand.

To set a standard, you must determine the *should* versus *must* parameter leaders. Jethro understood something many leaders miss. Don't be too rigid. *Should* suggests what ought to be done under regular circumstances but leaves open the possibility that unforeseen conditions may arise where a different path could be taken. No one set of rules can fully govern every situation your teams might face. Real leaders need direction and guidelines, not rails and shackles.

Embrace Leaders Who Will Leave the People Satisfied

We do not lead in a vacuum. We lead people. People have needs, feelings, personalities, and senses. People may be easily led like sheep at times, but even they will sniff out a wolf in sheep's clothing. If true and devoted people are not satisfied, this could be a sign you are lacking in your leadership at some level.

Think about this: "The stronger you are internally, the easier it becomes to be positively contagious in your leadership and the culture you're creating."[2]

It is not unusual to step into a new position and inherit the team someone else has gathered. Sometimes they are great and sometimes they are not. We will place new people into positions. Sometimes they work out as planned, and sometimes they do not. Some leaders just get frustrated. Some cause people to get fired, and some just accept the limitations and allow the organization to flounder. There is a fourth option to employ, and that is to help the team move forward. To do this the leader needs to have a tool to use to help the team to grow, not numerically but in the areas of competence, capacity, consistency, and creativity. This tool to help leaders grow is called expectation. Leadership expectations should be concise.

Concise Expectations

After years in both corporate life and church life, I have found one big difference. Churches usually do not have comprehensive, easy-to-remember expectations. And leaders are not incentivized on those expectations. I know some of you are thinking, *Sure we do, we have Ephesians 4; 1 Timothy 3 and 5; Titus 1; Hebrews 13; Acts 6; Exodus 18; and more!* That is my point. These are all great Scriptures, but condensing these ideas into a short, simple, memorable list helps leaders grow in the areas of execution and enthusiasm.

When I was looking for a pastoral opportunity coming out of seminary, I remember one church sending me their application, and I enthusiastically began the process of filling it in. By the time I got to the eighth page and the fifty-eighth question, I realized I was only a third of the way through. I am not exaggerating! I closed the application and threw it in the trash. I concluded that if they need to ask that many questions before even meeting me, I was the wrong man for the job.

Each of the Scriptures listed above has a list. Each of the lists is short. Why not stick to one of those lists for your church leaders rather than dump them all on them. Think about it. The original recipients of the lists only got one of the lists. Their list. Just because there are a lot of lists does not mean you have to focus your leaders on all of them. Pick one. Let the others serve as background support, or do as I did. Pick none of them, and let all of them serve as background support. That's right, you can create your own list with your own words that communicates the principles of all the other lists. My list for leaders had only three simple, short items.

1. Have a good reputation in the church and community.
2. Be regular in worship and Bible study.
3. Be a tither.

If ever asked, "What do you mean by this?" or "Why is this on the list?" then I would pull out Ephesians 4; 1 Timothy 3 and 5; Titus 1; Hebrews 13; Acts 6; Exodus 18, and any other Scriptures needed to answer the questions. Sure, in leaders meetings, conferences, Bible studies, and sermons, I taught from all of the Scriptures, but when expressing a list of requirements for leaders, I used a simplified list of three. And in all honesty, I was never asked the *what* or *why* questions because I believe the answers were self-evident.

Short, simple, concise lists are easy to remember. The ability to recall such a list makes it possible to focus efforts on the same. There is biblical precedent for this. In Exodus 20, Moses records the Ten Commandments given by God. The prophet Micah summarizes them in three,

"Mankind, he has told each of you what is good and what it is the LORD requires of you: to act justly, to love faithfulness, and to walk humbly with your God." (Mic. 6:8)

Later in the New Testament Jesus Himself further condenses them into two.

He said to him, "Love the Lord your God with all your heart, with all your soul, and with all your mind. This is the greatest and most important command. The second is like it: Love your neighbor as yourself. All the Law and the Prophets depend on these two commands." (Matt. 22:37–40)

On one occasion we were looking for someone to add to our deacon ministry. In a discussion with my deacon and trustee chairs, they suggested one of the men in our congregation. With a brisk shake of the head, I said, "He would not be able to serve in that leadership position." They asked why. My response was to remind them again of the three criteria we had in place for all leaders. The man they were suggesting had a good reputation, *check*, and was a tither, *check*, but he was not attending any Bible study.

It just so happened that when I left the office that day, guess who was in the church parking lot? That's right! The same gentleman offered up as a potential deacon. So I told him the leaders had just mentioned him as a possible new deacon. He smiled and straightened his posture as I spoke. Then I told him, "But you will never be a deacon here!" He asked why. "Because we have three criteria for all church leaders, and the one thing you are lacking is you do not attend any Bible study." You can guess what happened next. He started attending Bible study. In time he became the teacher of our senior high Sunday school class. He taught that class for fifteen consecutive years, rarely missing a Sunday. We entrusted to him a generation of students at that critical time in their lives as they were preparing to go off to college, the military, or start a career.

During those fifteen years, we did make him a deacon. And guess who was the chairman of the deacons at the time God called me away from the church to serve at Lifeway Christian Resources? Yes, it was him, Deacon Alexander Bess Jr. God used him to shepherd the church during that critical year as the church searched for a new pastor. Concise expectations really do make a difference.

Big results will not happen the day, month, or maybe even the year you begin setting the standard. Some things take time, patience, and consistency, but if you never set the standard, you will never see your team soar!

CHAPTER 12

Encourage the Team

Shepherd God's flock among you, not
overseeing out of compulsion but willingly,
as God would have you; not out of greed for
money but eagerly; not lording it over those
entrusted to you, but being examples to the
flock. And when the chief Shepherd appears,
you will receive the unfading crown of glory.
—1 Peter 5:2–4

Sometimes people only think about the job requirements. The truth is, when we take a secular job, we
are also concerned about the rewards. The pay, the
perks, and the place make a difference in our choices. When
it comes to encouraging the team, we must move from the
requirements to the rewards side of the equation.

The Bible gives us many leadership requirements, but
read the Bible further and be reminded that God also knows
we are motivated by rewards. Mark 10:29–30 says,

"Truly I tell you," Jesus said, "there is no one who has left house or brothers or sisters or mother or father or children or fields for my sake and for the sake of the gospel, who will not receive a hundred times more, now at this time—houses, brothers and sisters, mothers and children, and fields, with persecutions—and eternal life in the age to come."

God not only promises us heaven with Him, but He also reminds us of His eternal rewards systems. One of those systems uses crowns. Five crowns are mentioned in the Bible:

1. **The Crown of Glory.** This crown is for shepherding pastors and leaders who are willing, eager, and examples (1 Pet. 5:2–4).

2. **The Crown of Life.** This crown is given to "the one who endures trials" (James 1:12) and is "faithful to the point of death" (Rev. 2:10).

3. **The Crown of Rejoicing.** This crown is given to those who win the lost through evangelism (Phil. 4:1; 1 Thess. 2:19).

4. **The Crown of Righteousness.** This crown is promised "to all those who have loved his appearing," meaning those who

maintain a readiness for Christ's second coming (2 Tim. 4:8).

5. **The Incorruptible Crown.** This crown is awarded to everyone who "exercises self-control in everything" (1 Cor. 9:25).

Everybody needs the prospect of rewards to encourage them to keep going and to be their best. From the insufferable bondage of American slavery are the spirituals. One such song of encouragement is "Going to Shout All over God's Heav'n."[1]

> I've got a robe, you've got a robe,
> All of God's children got a robe.
> When I get to heaven goin' to put on my
> robe,
> goin' to shout all over God's heaven,
> heaven, heaven.
> Ev'rybody talking 'bout heaven ain't goin'
> there;
> heaven, heaven,
> goin' to shout all over God's heaven.

The ensuing verses all centered on things the slave had to suffer without here on this earth but hoped to receive in heaven—*shoes, wings, crown, harp, a song,* and even *a prayer.* Though we do not agree, it is not surprising that poorer people would gravitate to prosperity preachers who tell them they can *name it and claim it,* rather than wait for *pie in the sky, by and by, when we die.* This is all about hope and encouragement.

In the previous chapter we discussed concise expectations, but they also need to be celebrated if we want them to become contagious in the organizations. Celebration focused on expectations encourages the team to strive for excellence.

The Upwards Leader reports, "The fact is that people on your teams always need encouragement, that little boost daily to spur them on to better performance and to feel like they are appreciated in their work."[2]

Celebrate Expectation to Encourage

To determine or even declare the expectations is not enough. It is also not motivating if the only times we bring them up are when they have been in some way violated. Instead, we drive the importance and our commitment to the expectations by celebrating those who are achieving with consistency.

October is now celebrated by many churches as Pastor and Staff Appreciation Month. This is a great thing! First Timothy 5:17–18 directs us saying,

> The elders who are good leaders are to be considered worthy of double honor, especially those who work hard at preaching and teaching. For the Scripture says: Do

not muzzle an ox while it is treading out the grain, and, "The worker is worthy of his wages."

As true as this is for pastors and staff, remember, everyone likes appreciation, and a little positive reinforcement goes a long way. In the article, "Why Positive Encouragement Works Better Than Criticism,"[3] the writer informs us that "the emotional state of a leader can rub off on employees even when they're not sharing feedback specifically. Just being more upbeat can improve the emotional state of your employees, as well as helping them to be more efficient and coordinate better."

You can express encouragement in at least eight ways: saying good words, writing encouraging notes, verbally praying, supporting with tasks, touching, giving gifts, being present, and empathetic caring. Each of these can be employed to celebrate the expectations we have created for our teams.

The list of three are the minimum ones needed to do to be a leader. To celebrate the expectations, we added two more items and created the Quality Leader Award. This was a level of achievement each leader could ascribe to every year. The five criteria were:

1. Have a good reputation in the church and community.
2. Be regular in worship and Bible study.
3. Be a tither.

4. Attend two of our four Church Missional and Business Updates each year.

5. Complete and turn in an End of Year Leader Report and a Ministry Proposal Form on time each year.

By the way, if you are not *quality*, by implication, what are you? If you choose to do something like this, make sure your list items will help you develop the team you need and fulfill the vision you are seeking to achieve.

We would give out these awards to all the leaders who achieved *quality status* at a special dinner during our stewardship emphasis in November each year. The award included a gold medallion, a small gift, and a group photo with each name published in the church newsletter.

For this same event we asked all leaders to nominate one of their volunteer team members for a service award—someone who either really helped them accomplish their goals for the year or just needed encouragement. The award included a silver medallion, a small gift, and a group photo with each name published in the church newsletter.

In addition to these we developed:

- **Leader of Leaders Award.** This person would be a volunteer selected by the secret ballots of all the current leaders. The winner received a special certificate, a couple hundred dollars, a night on the town, and their name engraved

on an ongoing plaque hung on display at
the church.

- **Future Leader Award.** A teenager
  because of their work or potential would
  be selected by the secret ballots of all
  the current leaders. The winner received
  a couple hundred-dollar U.S. Savings
  Bond and their name engraved on an
  ongoing plaque hung on display at the
  church.

- **Team Spirit Award.** This went to the
  team/ministry that really worked
  together that year to achieve their goals.
  This team would be selected by the
  secret ballots of all the current leaders. The winning team leader received
  a Sunday breakfast in their honor and
  their ministry name engraved on an
  ongoing plaque hung on display at the
  church.

We stipulated for these latter three awards that no one
person or ministry could win two consecutive years. We
called the place where the plaques were located Heritage
Hall. From time to time, I would stand and read the names
and years on those plaques. As years passed, some of the
recipients were deceased and some, because of age, were
disabled. Some who were teens had become adults, making

good lives for themselves and their own contributions. I would read those names with humble appreciation because over the years the church had accomplished so much. The pastor often gets the credit, but truly what had been achieved could not have been accomplished absent the labors, leadership, and sacrifices of those whose names were listed on those plaques.

There is no way the church can accomplish all it does without the work of our volunteers, and there is no way we can pay any of our volunteers what they are worth for all they have contributed by their service, but a little appreciation goes a long way. These few dollars helped us energize an army of volunteers who were not working for the reward but were grateful that someone appreciated their efforts. A little celebration of the expectation helps our leaders get the big reward for King Jesus: "Well done, good and faithful servant!"

The Expectations We Celebrate Become Contagious

Raising the expectations for your leaders actually boosts the expectations for everyone. Generally speaking, church members believe pastors are supposed to do more. They are supposed to be more holy, more prayerful, more generous, more studious, and more faithful. They are expected to participate in worship, Bible study, prayer gatherings, evangelism events, mission projects, and even business meetings more faithfully. They perceive that it comes with the response to the call. They rationalize that since they do not have a "call" to ministry, they are less responsible, and being less committed is reasonable.

Something extraordinary that I was not anticipating happened when we consistently raised the expectations for our leaders and positively encouraged them. The majority of the members followed. For example, we had quarterly gatherings where our members could get detailed missional updates and insider information on the church's business activities and measures. These gatherings had been routinely small. Then we added attending these events to our annual Quality Leaders assessment. Most of our leaders started attending so they could achieve the Quality Leader status for the year. When their team members and others saw the leaders were now attending, they began to attend as well. These gatherings, which had been held in a classroom, eventually had to be moved to the sanctuary because it was the only space large enough to accommodate the crowd!

In his book *Contagious Leadership: 13 Principles to Spreading a Winning Culture*, Donte Hill reports, "As a leader you have to highlight the causes and passions that your team will scream about. Let them know why you are passionate about the company and/or the product that you are selling. Show them how they can get others excited. If your team is passionate about what your company is selling then customers will be too."[4]

No organization should want to be captive to mediocrity. This is exactly what happens, though, when we do not concisely and clearly communicate and celebrate the expectations for our leaders. However, once we do, they become contagious.

During 2020, we quarantined because we knew the deadly COVID-19 virus was contagious. Leadership excellence can be transmissible as well. Being infectious is not always bad. The World Economic Forum reports, "Good leaders increase employee engagement throughout their organization. Conversely, it also shows that ineffective senior managers decrease the engagement of their direct reports, and the people working for them, too."[5]

No wonder Paul speaks of the crowd of witnesses in Hebrews 11–12. Even when we are alone, they are cheering and encouraging us to keep going!

➤ Leadership Team Questions ◄

1. What are the strengths of the members of your team?

2. What are the weaknesses of the members of your team?

3. What additional skills does your team need to meet the needs of your church?

4. How are you communicating your expectations for the team?

5. What are the things you need to implement to improve and encourage your team?

Epilogue

The hard thing when you get old is to keep your horizons open. The first part of your life everything is in front of you, all your potential and promise. But over the years, you make decisions; you carve yourself into a given shape. Then the challenge is to keep discovering the green growing edge.
—Howard Thurman[1]

A dream doesn't become reality through magic; it takes sweat, determination and hard work.
—General Colin Powell[2]

Goals are pure fantasy unless you have a specific plan to achieve them.
—Stephen Covey[3]

Dream the dream. Plan the plan. Execute the plan. Live the dream.
—Rick Thomason[4]

For I am already being poured out as a drink offering, and the time for my departure is close. I have fought the good fight, I have finished the race, I have kept the faith. There is reserved for me the crown of righteousness, which the Lord, the righteous Judge, will give me on that day, and not only to me, but to all those who have loved his appearing.
—2 Timothy 4:6–8

CHAPTER 13

Go for the Biggest of the Big Results

His master said to him, "Well done, good
and faithful servant! You were faithful over
a few things; I will put you in charge of
many things. Share your master's joy."
—Matthew 25:23

I hate fruitless efforts. I loathe spending an abundance of time and energy on a task and achieving little to nothing. The apostle Paul expressed this sentiment in 1 Corinthians 9:27. He said, "Instead, I discipline my body and bring it under strict control, so that after preaching to others, I myself will not be disqualified." In Philippians 3:12–14, toward the end of his life, on a forced retirement from a stellar career, under house arrest, with a death sentence looming, he declared,

> Not that I have already reached the goal or
> am already perfect, but I make every effort

to take hold of it because I also have been taken hold of by Christ Jesus. Brothers and sisters, I do not consider myself to have taken hold of it. But one thing I do: Forgetting what is behind and reaching forward to what is ahead, I pursue as my goal the prize promised by God's heavenly call in Christ Jesus.

I love that! That unquenchable fire in the belly that wants to give it all to the end, leaving nothing on the field, that passion to live life, unwilling to look back with a pile of regretful could of, should of, and would of.

Jesus had that passion. We see it summarized in James Allan Francis's poem, "One Solitary Life."[1]

> He was born in an obscure village
> The child of a peasant woman
> He grew up in still another village
> Where he worked in a carpenter shop
> Until he was thirty when public opinion
> turned against him
>
> He never wrote a book
> He never held an office
> He never went to college
> He never visited a big city
> He never travelled more than two hundred
> miles

GO FOR THE BIGGEST OF THE BIG RESULTS

From the place where he was born
He did none of the things
Usually associated with greatness
He had no credentials but himself

He was only thirty-three

His friends ran away
One of them denied him
He was turned over to his enemies
And went through the mockery of a trial
He was nailed to a cross between two
thieves.
While dying, his executioners gambled for
his clothing
The only property he had on earth.

When he was dead
He was laid in a borrowed grave
Through the pity of a friend.

Nineteen centuries have come and gone
And today he is the central figure of the
human race
And the leader of mankind's progress
All the armies that ever marched
All the navies that ever sailed
All the parliaments that ever sat
All the kings that ever reigned put together
Have not affected the life of mankind on earth
As powerfully as that one solitary life.

Habit 2 in Stephen Covey's 7 *Habits of Highly Effective People* is to "begin with the end in mind."[2] That is what Jesus did. That is what we must also do.

Toward the end of the Gospel recorded by Matthew, Jesus gives us some pointed guidance about how to approach the end. In Matthew 25, it is the end of time, but allow us to think in terms of the end of *our* time. There are three parables in this chapter. Permit me to suggest that they speak to three things that are vital for each of us to end with big results. Simply expressed, they are our moments, methods, and motives. Moments are when we do what we do. Methods are how we realize our accomplishments. Motives are the why that drives us behind it all.

Big Results Moments

Moments are just that, transitory, fleeting instances of time that come and go. We must choose what we do as kairotic seasons arise prayerfully. The decisions we make and the paths we take, in those times, can make a world of difference.

It is the impact of our use of a moment that we get to glimpse in Matthew 25:1–13, the parable of the ten virgins. The parable begins, "At that time the kingdom of heaven will be like ten virgins who took their lamps and went out to meet the groom. . . . The wise ones took oil in their flasks with their lamps."

I want to draw your attention to the five wise virgins who were ready for the moment. The five foolish ones were not. We never read every detail of the lives of the heroes and heroines of faith in the Bible. Only flashing glimpses of their significant moments are recorded. Moments like Noah's moment with the ark, Moses' moment with Pharaoh, David's moment with Goliath, Job's moment of suffering, Peter's moment on Pentecost, and Jesus' moment on the cross. These scenes are not the sum total of all they are or all they had accomplished. John ends his Gospel with the words,

> This is the disciple who testifies to these things and who wrote them down. We know that his testimony is true. And there are also many other things that Jesus did, which, if every one of them were written down, I suppose not even the world itself could contain the books that would be written. (John 21:24–25)

Martin Luther King Jr., in his book *Strength to Love*, said, "The ultimate measure of a man is not where he stands in moments of convenience and comfort, but where he stands at times of challenge and controversy."[3] Dr. Benjamin E. Mays, who served a nearly three-decade tenure as the sixth president of Morehouse College, a historically black institution of higher learning in Atlanta, Georgia, is credited with writing and often quoting the poem "I Have Only Just a Minute."[4]

I have only just a minute,
Only sixty seconds in it.
Forced upon me, can't refuse it.
Didn't seek it, didn't choose it.
But it's up to me to use it.

I must suffer if I lose it.
Give account if I abuse it.
Just a tiny little minute,
but eternity is in it.

To achieve big results, moments matter. Our lives are made up of moments. We must anticipate the moments, be ready for the moments, seize the moments, and when necessary, rise to the moments.

Big Results Methods

When I was in school, I read a small book called *The Prince*. It was written by Niccolò Machiavelli in the year AD 1532. This classic ultimately concludes "the end justifies the means." He states in chapter 8, "One ascends to the principality by some wicked or nefarious ways."[5] Later, in *The Discourses*, Machiavelli writes, "For although the act condemns the doer, the end may justify him."[6] Machiavelli's argument was if the goal is good, then we are free to use whatever means necessary to achieve it. Leaders must be careful not to unwittingly believe and follow this philosophy. The apostle Paul says, "What should we say then? Should we continue in sin so that grace may multiply? Absolutely not! How can we who died to sin still live in it?" (Rom. 6:1–2.) Thus, the end never justifies the means. If the goal is good, the process to achieve it must be also.

The second parable in Matthew 25:14–28 is the parable of the talents. Here three servants are all given talents. The first servant five, the second two, and the third one, *depending on each one's ability*. These are no small investments. One talent was worth about twenty years' wages.[7] So it is like these servants are essentially given a lifetime's wages all in a lump sum at the beginning of their working year. Could you imagine if that were you? How would it impact your life? What would you do differently?

The first servant with five talents works, buys, trades, sells, and invests. And when he gives an account, he is able to report double for his trouble. The master is happy and gives the servant a promotion. The second servant does the same and turns two talents into four. The master is ecstatic and also puts this servant in charge of more. The problem is with the third servant. He was afraid in verse 25. So, rather than use the proven and commonly understood methods that bring him success, he hid the one talent he was given.

What's most interesting to me here is the servant with the one talent gives it back to the master at the accounting in total. That's right. He gives back 100 percent, all of it.

Not a penny was taken away. Yet not only is the master not pleased, but he calls the servant evil, lazy, and good-for-nothing. He demands that at least he should have received bank interest on his money. To add injury to this insult, the master takes the one talent from the servant and gives it to the servant who already has the most. The lazy servant is then thrown into "the outer darkness, where there will be weeping and gnashing of teeth" (v. 30).

Many lessons can be drawn from this parable, but let us glean this one: God expects us to faithfully execute the proven methods that will leave whatever He has put in our charge bigger, or at least better. It should not die on our watch. We cannot see ourselves as maintenance personnel. It is not good enough to leave it just as it was when we arrived. God has placed us for a purpose. He expects us to do something: to move, grow, build, expand, achieve, change, shift, transform, add, develop, and/or mature something.

We see this here with God's servant Paul while on house arrest and facing a death sentence.

> Not that I have already reached the goal or am already perfect, but I make every effort to take hold of it because I also have been taken hold of by Christ Jesus. Brothers and sisters, I do not consider myself to have taken hold of it. But one thing I do: Forgetting what is behind and reaching forward to what is ahead, I pursue as my goal

the prize promised by God's heavenly call in
Christ Jesus. (Phil. 3:12–14)

Paul writes these words to the Philippian church
because there are some Antinomians in the community.
The Antinomians believed there was no need to achieve
anything. They believed God would forgive us and accept
any and everything we do and offer to him. Like the wicked
servant, the Antinomians were complaisant. Paul here
encourages us to forget previous accomplishments and use
the potential within.

Paul had to forget his three missionary journeys. He
had already started churches all over Asia Minor. He could
not settle for the great offering he collected and took to
Jerusalem; his efforts to broaden the appeal of the gospel
and to take it to the Gentiles; the times he had been ship-
wrecked, stoned, beaten, and abused; the wife he lost and
the children he never took time to have; his hungry days and
his sleepless nights; the achievements his training and pedi-
gree could have brought him; or the lucrative tent-making
business he had to abandon for the gospel's sake.

Paul forgets all these things and writes in the last days
of his life. He writes the Philippian letter in jail on a forced
retirement from a stellar career. No longer able to travel,
he could have become antinomianistically complacent. But
instead, he writes letters and sends emissaries. He does
this from a prison cell. This part of his work has been most
remembered, appreciated, and most influential. He reminds

us that even if our task is not easy, our method is to remain faithful.

Whether you are assigned to a small ministry in the country or mega ministry in the city; if your church is one hundred years old or one hundred days old; if the members are rich or poor, high level of education or low level of common sense; powerful or easily beguiled; as a pastor, politician, parent, partner, professor, or pal, be faithful.

Having served my first church for more than a quarter of a century, I can testify that the first few years can lay a foundation for a long, loving, fruitful, and fulfilling relationship between pastor and people. Ironically, my seminary training didn't teach me the five key strategies that led to twenty-six years of fellowshipping with a congregation who became my second family. Allow me to share what I believe can help you do the same.[8]

1. Learn

You may have completed the seminary curriculum, but you are only beginning the church's. Get to know the people, the church—its history, personality, and culture—and the community. When I went to my first church, it was ninety-nine years old, and everything was running well. Other than preparing my sermons, I didn't know what to do. So I spent a lot of time visiting members and getting to know people in the community. As Ezekiel began his ministry, he "sat there among them stunned for seven days" (Ezek. 3:15). Every church and community are different. Just like you exegete the biblical text, you must exegete your church and community if you really want to know them.

2. Commit

Don't you hate it when you are at a large event and the person shaking your hand is already looking at the next person he or she wants to greet? Just as the universal church is the bride of Christ, as Christ's representative the local church is like the pastor's bride, as well. And just as no bride wants her husband looking longingly at another woman, your church wants to know if you will be committed. Commitment in this kind of relationship means you are willing to hang in there even if times get tough. I think that if a church does not have a crisis, it will create one to find out if you have what it takes to stay. Close the personal back door, stop looking for your next ministry assignment, and commit to staying until God says otherwise.

3. Press

My mother reminded me in those early years that the church is not the speedboat but the Old Ship of Zion, and it takes a while to turn a ship. Honor the good things from the past. Those things were good for *that* time, but you live in *this* time. Maintain a kingdom focus and press forward in a patient way. Find one thing the church has wanted to accomplish, and make it happen! Honoring their desires first will help get them on board for what God is telling you about the church's future.

That being said, remember some things never change. I stood at the helm of one such old ship, and twenty-six years later not everything has changed. Not everything, but enough things changed. Not everything, but the important things changed.

4. Stand

Stand on God's Word in a firm but humble way. Once our church wanted to do something that was acceptable in the church constitution but violated the Word of God. I stood on the Word. I believe there will be times as a pastor that you cannot do your job unless you are willing to lose your job. Colossians 3:23–24 says,

> Whatever you do, do it from the heart, as something done for the Lord and not for people, knowing that you will receive the reward of an inheritance from the Lord. You serve the Lord Christ.

Second Timothy 4:16–17 reminds us of the apostle Paul,

> At my first defense, no one stood by me, but everyone deserted me. May it not be counted against them. But the Lord stood with me and strengthened me, so that I might fully preach the word and all the Gentiles might hear it. So I was rescued from the lion's mouth.

5. Refresh

Never let the ministry become just a job, or the preaching just a task, or worship just a calendar event, or prayer just a ritual. Keep your mind, your heart, and your relationship with God, and your love for God, fresh. You will be faced with all kinds of days, seasons, situations, and experiences in long-term leadership. As members become friends and family over the years and as they face financial, family, health, and other crises, you will carry them along with your flesh-and-blood and personal issues. The care of the saints can wear you out if you let it. "The joy of the LORD is your strength" (Neh. 8:10) has to become more than a cute Bible verse. It has to become the reality of your life.

What you preach to and teach others week after week and year after year has to be refreshment for you as well as your people; it should never be just for *them*. Disconnect, take time off—the church will keep going without you. Love God first, love the people second. Jesus said,

> "The one who loves a father or mother more
> than me is not worthy of me; the one who
> loves a son or daughter more than me is not
> worthy of me." (Matt. 10:37)

Refresh yourself so you can bring your best self to this most important task. If you do these things, and start doing them early, you can make sure you are there long enough to get big results!

Big Results Motives

Once when I was about eight years old, I went grocery shopping with my mother. One of the benefits of such an excursion was that if I did a good job, when we got to the checkout counter, I might be able to get some snack. You know how the stores always put little sweets and irresistible treats near the checkout counters. At Glen's Market there were devil's food cupcakes with no icing, but filled with vanilla cream, called Yankee Doodles. They were one of my favorites. On this particular shopping excursion, my mom blessed me with a pack of Yankee Doodles. I gently laid them on the top of the bag as I packed the groceries. I made sure they did not fall out as we walked four blocks home. I set them on the kitchen table as I helped put everything away. Then it was time. I could get a glass of milk and sit down to enjoy my treasure.

However, something I was not anticipating happened. My grandmother was there. She saw my Yankee Doodles and asked me for one. Excuse me?! I didn't know what to do. I wanted them so much that I felt I needed all three of them, but I also knew I could not say no to Nana. So with bitter reluctance I grabbed one and handed it in her direction with a short, "Here!"

Nana refused it. She told me my motives were wrong, and if I could not offer it in love, she did not want it. On the bright side, I got my Yankee Doodle back and got to eat all three. But on the other hand, I could not enjoy them because I had disappointed my grandmother by having the wrong motives.

Our motives do make a difference. It is never good enough just to do the right thing. We must also do it for the right reasons. With God our motives count. Proverbs 21:2 says, "All a person's ways seem right to him, but the LORD weighs hearts." Ephesians 6:6 also proclaims, "Don't work only while being watched, as people pleasers, but as slaves of Christ, do God's will from your heart."

In the third parable in Matthew 25, verses 31–46, it never ceases to amaze me what the people did not know. The king shares his gratitude for the people's service to him when he was thirsty, a stranger, naked, sick, and a prisoner, but the people are totally caught off guard and unaware. "Then the righteous will answer him, 'Lord, when did we see you hungry and feed you, or thirsty and give you something to drink? When did we see you a stranger and take you in, or without clothes and clothe you? When did we see you sick, or in prison, and visit you?'" (Matt. 25:37–39).

What I see as a beautiful thing in this exchange is that the righteous are totally unaware that they were doing something special for the king. They were just doing good because it was a natural part of their lives. They were not looking for a reward. They were not trying to gain brownie points, nor were they trying to get on somebody's good side. Their motives were pure. They were just being themselves, doing what was right, and doing good.

Big results are about kingdom impact, not merely personal aggrandizement. Bigger is not necessarily better. Just to be big is not the goal of big results. Big can never be a goal in and of itself. Our ultimate goal ought always to be the glory of Almighty God.

Glory is an interesting churchy word. The Hebrew word is *shekinah*. In Greek it is *doxa*. It reminds me that we are never to seek or take credit for anything because without God we could not accomplish anything.

Ecclesiastes 2:24–26 says,

> There is nothing better for a person than to eat, drink, and enjoy his work. I have seen that even this is from God's hand, because who can eat and who can enjoy life apart from him? For to the person who is pleasing in his sight, he gives wisdom, knowledge, and joy; but to the sinner he gives the task of gathering and accumulating in order to give to the one who is pleasing in God's sight. This too is futile and a pursuit of the wind.

So to give God glory, whenever people tell us how great they think we are or how wonderful are our accomplishments, we must tell the truth. None of us had any big results on our own. Giving glory to God, we willingly step out of the spotlight and shine the light on God. We do not deserve any credit. We were merely instruments managed by the Almighty. Only in Him are the biggest of the big results.

All glory and honor belong to God the Father, Son, and Holy Spirit.

World without end. Amen.

➤ Leadership Biggest Questions ◄

1. What have been the most transformational moments during your life in your childhood?

> Adult life?
>
> Leadership position or career?
>
> County and world?

2. What Scriptures do you use to remind yourself to use God-honoring methods?

3. What is the most important thing to you in leadership? What is your real underlying motive?

4. What do you want people to remember about you and your leadership when you are done?

Notes

Introduction

1. D. T. Hall and D. E. Chandler, "Psychological Success: When the Career Is a Calling," *Journal of Organizational Behavior*, 26 (2005), 160.

Part 1: Study

1. Jon Acuff, *Do Over: Make Today the First Day of Your New Career* (Portfolio, 2017).

Chapter 1: What Did I Just Get Into?

1. They had been in Egypt for 430 years (Exod. 12:40–41), minus the time until a pharaoh who knew not Joseph (Exod. 1:8) equals 400 years in slavery (Gen. 15:13 and Acts 7:6).

2. All uses of Google Maps and Google Earth Content must provide attribution to both Google and our data providers. We do not approve of any use of content without proper attribution, in any circumstance. But within those limits, Google says, you can use images in reports, presentations, on the web, in a print project.

3. "Mosaic® USA Customer Segmentation Solution," Experian, https://www.experian.com/marketing-services/consumer-segmentation.

4. Numbers 13:33

5. https://lyricsplayground.com/alpha/songs/t/thewaywewere.html

6. Danielle Dahl, "50 Eeyore Quotes to Make You Smile and Think," Everyday Power, https://everydaypower.com/eeyore-quotes.

7. "Three of the World's Fastest Speed Boats," Cox, November 26, 2019, https://www.coxmarine.com/3-of-the-worlds-fastest-speed-boats.

Chapter 2: Gain a Passion for the People

1. *Native American Encyclopedia.*
2. LaMar Eugene Cooper, *Ezekiel,* The New American Commentary, Volume 17 (Nashville: Holman Reference, 1994).
3. Matthew 6:10

Chapter 3: Find the Motivation

1. "Vegetarian Diet: How to Get the Best Nutrition," Mayo Clinic, https://www.mayoclinic.org/healthy-lifestyle/nutrition-and -healthy-eating/in-depth/vegetarian-diet/art-20046446.
2. "All about Icebergs," Beyond Penguins and Polar Bears, OSU.EDU, https://beyondpenguins.ehe.osu.edu/issue/icebergs-and -glaciers/all-about-icebergs.
3. R. M. Ryan and E. L. Deci, "Intrinsic and Extrinsic Motivations," *Contemporary Educational Psychology,* 25 (2000), 54–67.

Part 2: Vision

1. Stephen R. Covey, *7 Habits of Highly Effective People* (Salt Lake City: FranklinCovey, 1989), 95.
2. "Helen Keller Quotes about Vision," AZ Quotes, https://www .azquotes.com/author/7843-Helen_Keller/tag/vision.
3. John Maxwell, *Intentional Living: Choosing a Life that Matters* (Reprint ed., New York: Center Street, 2017).
4. "58 Thought-Provoking Quotes by Howard Thurman for the Theologians," The Famous People, https://quotes.thefamouspeople .com/howard-thurman-4832.php.
5. "Quotes on Reaching Life and Leadership Goals, ConantLeadership, October 28, 2016, https://conantleadership .com/37-quotes-life-leadership-goals.

Chapter 4: Get a Vision

1. Bill Hybels, *Who You Are When No One's Looking: Choosing Consistency, Resisting Compromise* (Downers Grove, IL: IVP, 1987), 35.
2. "The Impossible Dream," *Man of La Mancha,* Songwriters: Joe Darion / Mitchell Leigh, 1965.
3. *Strong's Talking Greek and Hebrew Dictionary,* 1798.
4. "Martin Luther King, Jr.," American Rhetoric, https://www .americanrhetoric.com/speeches/mlkivebeentothemountaintop.htm.

Chapter 5: Cast the Vision

1. H. Franklin Paschall and Herschel H. Hobbs, eds., *The Teacher's Bible Commentary: A Concise, Thorough Interpretation of the Entire Bible Designed Especially for Sunday School Teachers* (Nashville: B&H Academic, 1972).

Chapter 6: Wait for It

1. *Book of Jasher* 44:76.

Part 3: Execute

1. Morris Change, "Strategy Execution," The Leadership Group, http://theleadershipgroup.asia/service/strategy-execution.

2. Asad Meah, "46 Inspirational Gary Vaynerchuk Quotes on Success," January 12, 2017, https://www.awakenthegreatnesswithin .com/46-inspirational-gary-vaynerchuk-quotes-on-success.

3. "Christian Nestell Bovee Quotes," Citatis, accessed March 2, 2021, https://citatis.com/a10019/115066.

4. Kitkatpersons, "Grandma's Marathon: 2016 Reflection," Saltspiration, June 27, 2016, https://saltspiration.wordpress.com /2016/06.

Chapter 7: Make a Decision

1. Avery Hartmans, "Airbnb Now Has More Listings Worldwide than the Top Five Hotel Brands Combined," *Business Insider*, August 10, 2017, https://www.businessinsider.com/airbnb-total-worldwide -listings-2017-8#:~:text=The%20San%20Francisco%2Dbased%20 startup,%2C%20Spain%2C%20and%20the%20UK.

2. Minda Zetlin, "Blockbuter Could Have Bought Netflix," *Inc.*, accessed March 2, 2021, https://www.inc.com/minda-zetlin/net-flix-blockbuster-meeting-marc-randolph-reed-hastings-john-antioco .html.

3. Ariel Shapiro, "Netflix Stock Hits Record High, Is Now Worth More Than Disney," *Forbes*, April 16, 2020, https://www.forbes.com/ sites/arielshapiro/2020/04/16/netflix-stock-hits-record-high-is-now -worth-more-than-disney/#5f0b6a644b26.

4. Charles Wesley, "A Charge to Keep I Have," 1762, Timeless Truths, https://library.timelesstruths.org/music/A_Charge _to_Keep_I_Have.

Chapter 8: Make Progress

1. "Cliff Young (athlete)," Wikipedia, https://en.wikipedia.org/wiki/Cliff_Young_(athlete).

2. "Cliffy," IMBd, accessed March 2, 2021, https://www.imdb.com/title/tt2169274.

3. John Donne, "No Man Is an Island," https://web.cs.dal.ca/~johnston/poetry/island.html.

4. "Martin Luther King," *Los Angeles Times*, January 19, 1998, https://www.latimes.com/archives/la-xpm-1998-jan-19-me-10002-story.html.

5. "'People,' Barbra Streisand," Lyrics, https://www.lyrics.com/lyric/356776/Barbra+Streisand/People.

6. "A Man May Do an Immense Deal of Good, if He Does Not Care Who Gets the Credit," Quote Investigator, https://quoteinvestigator.com/2010/12/21/doing-good-selfless.

7. "Chirk (up)," Merriam-Webster, https://www.merriam-webster.com/thesaurus/chirk.

8. Joseph Luciani, "Why 80 Percent of New Year's Resolutions Fail," *U. S. News*, December 29, 2015, https://health.usnews.com/health-news/blogs/eat-run/articles/2015-12-29/why-80-percent-of-new-years-resolutions-fail.

9. Sean Covey, Jim Huling, and Chris McChesney, *The 4 Disciplines of Execution: Achieving Your Wildly Important Goals* (Sal Lake City: FranklinCovey, 2012).

10. Gary Keller, *The One Thing* (Austin, TX: Bard Press, 2021), 170–80.

Chapter 9: Make Friends, Make Enemies

1. "The Story of *The 5 Love Languages®*," The 5 Love Languages, https://www.5lovelanguages.com/5-love-languages.

2. "99 Great Quotes that Will Help You Handle Criticism," Lolly Daskal, https://www.lollydaskal.com/leadership/99-great-quotes-that-will-help-you-handle-criticism/ #77.

3. Ibid., #70.

4. Paul Pressler, *A Hill on Which to Die: One Southern Baptist's Journey* (Nashville: B&H Publishing Group, 1999), 297.

Part 4: Team

1. Megan Conley, "45 Quotes That Celebrate Teamwork, Hard Work, and Collaboration," HubSpot, https://blog.hubspot.com/marketing/teamwork-quotes.
2. John C. Maxwell, *The 17 Indisputable Laws of Teamwork: Embrace Them and Empower Your Team* (New York: HarperCollins Leadership, 2013), 57.

Chapter 10: Build a Team

1. "The Ant Colony: Structure and Roles," *Western Exterminator Company*, https://www.westernexterminator.com/ants/the-ant-colony-structure-and-roles.

Chapter 11: Set the Standard

1. Tom Ziglar, "If You Aim at Nothing . . . ," Ziglar, https://www.ziglar.com/articles/if-you-aim-at-nothing-2.
2. Anese Cavanaugh, *Contagious Culture: Show Up, Set the Tone, and Intentionally Create an Organization that Thrives* (New York: McGraw-Hill Education, 2016), 110.

Chapter 12: Encourage the Team

1. Public domain
2. Paul LaRue, "The Benefits of Encouragement," *The Upwards Leader*, https://upwardsleader.com/2015/01/21/the-benefits-of-encouragement.
3. Belle Beth Cooper, "Why Positive Encouragement Works Better Than Criticism," *Fast Company*, https://www.fastcompany.com/3025080/why-positive-encouragement-works-better-than-criticism - :~:text=Just being more upbeat can,the negativity among other employees.
4. Donte Hill, *Contagious Leadership: 13 Principles to Spreading a Winning Culture* (Scotts Valley, CA: CreateSpace, 2011), 69.
5. Rosamund Hutt, "Is Good Leadership Contagious?," World Economic Forum, February 8, 2016, https://www.weforum.org/agenda/2016/02/is-leadership-contagious.

Epilogue

1. "58 Thought-Provoking Quotes by Howard Thurman for the Theologians," https://quotes.thefamouspeople.com/howard-thurman-4832.php.

2. "37 Quotes on Reaching Life and Leadership Goals," ConantLeadership, October 28, 2016, https://conantleadership.com/37-quotes-life-leadership-goals.

3. "Stephen Covey Quotes," QuoteTab, https://www.quotetab.com/quote/by-stephen-covey/stop-setting-goals-goals-are-pure-fantasy-unless-you-have-a-specific-plan-to-achieve.

4. "How to Kick the Bucket in Style. Have a 2021 Buckeet List?" December 17, 2020, https://www.zmazh.com/2021_kick-the-bucket .

Chapter 13: Go for the Biggest of the Big Results

1. James Allan Francis, "One Solitary Life," All Poetry, 1926, https://allpoetry.com/poem/12152369-One-Solitary-Life-Made-A-Difference--by-Ed-ostrom.

2. Stephen R. Covey, 7 Habits of Highly Effective People (Salt Lake City: FranklinCovey, 1989), 95.

3. Martin Luther King Jr., Strength to Love (Minneapolis: Fortress Press, 2010), 1963.

4. Poem by Dr. Benjamin E. Mays, "I Have Only Just a Minute," public domain.

5. Niccolò Machiavelli, The Prince (New York: Penguin Classics, 2003), chapter 8.

6. Niccolò Machiavelli, The Discourses (Abu Dhabi: Royal Classics, 2020), I, 9.

7. John D. Barry, et al., "Talent," The Lexham Bible Dictionary (Mariton, NJ: Lexham Press, 2016).

8. "Turning Your New Pastorate into a Long-Term Pastorate, Lifeway Research, July 17, 2018, accessed March 6, 2021, https://factsandtrends.net/2018/07/17/turning-your-new-pastorate-into-a-long-term-pastorate.